CAN YOU BELIEVE THESE MIND-BOGGLERS?

—The two-headed man who argued with himself?
—The animal that defeated a vast army of rats alone?
—The fighter who killed 1425 opponents?
—The flower that predicts weather?
—The viper that hunts with radar?
—The three-legged football player?
—The nine-year-old girl who wrote a bestselling novel?
—The creature that lived underground for seventeen years?
—The housewife who won four Olympic gold medals?
—The city that contains four hundred temples?
—The marine who did 17,000 consecutive sit-ups?

This is the book that will make you a believer—in how amazing reality can be when you venture beyond the borders of the ordinary to explore the most far-out realms of the remarkable.

More Incredible!

by

Kevin McFarland

Illustrated by Luis Dominguez

A SIGNET BOOK

NEW AMERICAN LIBRARY

TIMES MIRROR

Contents

Sohn glided to earth on canvas wings from almost four miles up

Man has always been intrigued by the thought of flying through his own physical power, without the aid of any heavy mechanism. The man who has come closest to that dream was Clem Sohn.

Sohn, an air-show performer in the 1930's, had perfected a way of gliding through the air with home-made wings. He had himself dropped from an airplane at a height of approximately 20,000 feet, and then he would float downward some three miles or so until he was but 800 or 1,000 feet from the ground, at which point he would open up his parachute for the final descent.

Clem, who hailed from Lansing, Michigan, made his wings out of zephyr cloth and mounted them on steel tubes to form a large web which was clasped to his hips. A loose cloth formed another web between his legs. His large goggles gave him an appearance which justifiably led to his becoming known as *"The Batman."*

Sohn's amazing act came to an end on April 25, 1937, in Vincennes, France. Before taking off, Clem had remarked, "I feel as safe as you would in your grandmother's kitchen." But during his descent on that day, his parachute didn't open. A terror-stricken crowd of 100,000 watched him frantically tug on the ripcord of his emergency chute, but that failed, too; and Clem Sohn, only 26 years old, plunged to his death.

The Eiffel Tower is the tallest structure in Europe

In the late 1880's, the city of Paris was swept by a storm of protest over a planned tower for the upcoming International Exposition. The proposed structure—intended to symbolize the glory of France—was decried by artists, writers, and officials alike as a use-less monstrosity, an affront to the history of great monuments in its use of the then despised material, steel. Yet, despite these pro-tests, the pressures of time, and a limited knowledge of the necessary structural techniques, Alexander Gustave Eiffel pressed on with his design. Almost 90 years later, this structure—the Eiffel

2

Tower—is the highest (excluding TV towers), grandest, and most famous tower in the world, and the symbol of a nation.

The tallest structure in Europe (again, excluding TV towers, navigational masts, and chimneys), the Eiffel Tower rises 1,052 feet over a long landscaped promenade near the River Seine. At its base, four huge masonry pillars anchor four steel columns, which join at a height of 620 feet to form one slender spire. A football field could be placed between these pillars with room to spare.

Construction of the massive tower was completed in only 17 months, in time for the International Exposition of 1889. The design, a combination of the arch and the obelisk, called for the use of 12,000 component parts weighing a total of 7,500 tons. Despite the lack of sophisticated safety measures, there were no fatal accidents during the entire period of construction. Equally surprising, the total cost of over $1 million was recovered from sightseers within *one year!*

Today, the Eiffel Tower is one of the most popular tourist attractions in the world. Elevators rise aslant along the columns to observation decks at three levels, which provide a vista of Paris and the surrounding countryside up to 90 miles away!

Although the tower was decried as useless from its very inception, from 1925 to 1936 it supported the largest advertising sign ever erected. This electric "Citroen" sign, consisting of 250,000 lamps, was visible from as far as 24 miles away. Today, the Eiffel functions as a radio and TV broadcast tower, a meteorological station, and of course, as France's greatest tourist attraction.

Salmon will fight a current for one thousand miles

Of all the earth's sea creatures, the salmon is the finest and most determined navigator. This remarkable fish will swim great distances against a current to spawn in the precise stream in which it was born.

Salmon mature in the ocean, often growing to a length of four feet within one or two years. But at the appropriate season, depending on the species, they suddenly seek out freshwater and begin swimming upstream. During this frenzied upriver climb, salmon will buck a current and swim at thirty miles an hour, fighting rapids and leaping waterfalls as high as fifteen feet—no small feat for a fish that often weighs over seventy pounds. Their silvery scales turn a characteristic red as they hurry through rivers and streams, never pausing, not even to eat.

For most salmon, the journey does not end until the fish has found the stream in which it was born. Some of these extraordinary creatures have journeyed the length of the Yukon River to find their natal stream—a voyage of over one thousand miles. How do they find their way? Incredible as it may seem, experiments have shown that spawning salmon locate the right stream by
4

means of a highly developed sense of smell! When the salmon arrive, they lay their eggs in gravel pits in the stream bed. Their duty done, many of the Pacific species then die, never to return to the sea again—although other species do survive a return trip.

Some of the young salmon that are born in these streams will descend immediately to the ocean; others—like the sockeye salmon—will live for as long as five years in freshwater before journeying downstream to the sea. And eventually each salmon will return once more to this parent stream.

⚬⚭⚬

Alvin York captured 130 German prisoners by himself at one time

It was on October 8, 1918 that a small group of American soldiers were surrounded by Germans in the Argonne Forest of France. On all sides were German machine-gun nests. The wounded sergeant of the troop, unable to continue, passed command to a young corporal named Alvin York. Capture seemed imminent. But the boy from Fentress County, Tennessee did not give up. In-

stead he stood up and, flattening his body against a tree, began to fire. Twelve Germans fell in short order. In stark amazement and fury, eight Germans charged down a hill at the lone American soldier. York fired eight times and slew all eight. The other Germans, not knowing that they had surrounded a handful of American soldiers, thought that they *themselves* were outmanned. They abandoned their positions to surrender.

Soon York discovered that he had captured *92 prisoners.* The six Americans under York's command were really in a spot: they were in German territory, and they were vastly outnumbered by their prisoners. But again, young York was equal to the task. He marched the prisoners ahead of him, toward the American lines. Whenever they came to another German machine-gun nest, the gunners assumed that a large army battalion was behind the group of prisoners walking toward them. By the time York reached the American lines, he had collected 132 prisoners and had put out of action 35 machine-gun nests. He later received the highest governmental awards from the U.S. and France.

⟨∞∾∾⟩

Menuhin was a great violinist at 11

When Yehudi Menuhin was 11 years old, he was hailed by many music experts as the most gifted natural violinist ever to have appeared on the concert stage. Wearing shorts and an open shirt, he performed Beethoven's "Violin Concerto," accompanied by the New York Philharmonic Orchestra. His technical virtuosity and musical insight was such that both critics and public could hardly believe their ears. Even members of the orchestra wept.

The son of a chicken farmer and a schoolteacher, Menuhin achieved world fame with a minimum of musical training. In fact, his violin instructors were so overwhelmed by the effortless purity of his playing that they hesitated to meddle with his style at all. Menuhin played classical compositions at the age of four, and made his stage debut with the San Francisco Symphony Orchestra at seven.

Nor was the young Yehudi's genius restricted to the stage. As a boy he could also read such classic writers as Dante in Italian and Descartes in French.

Now nearing 50, Menuhin remains one of the world's great violinists. Unlike many prodigies, he has grown up to be both a happy and successful adult. Still, there are critics who say that with maturity Menuhin has lost some of the natural beauty of style he exhibited as a child genius.

Benjamin Franklin was the most versatile man who ever lived

Benjamin Franklin said, "I wish the good Lord had seen fit to make the day twice as long as it is. Perhaps then I could *really* accomplish something."

Thus spoke this many-sided man who did any number of things—and did them all amazingly well. He was a painter, writer, publisher, scientist, statesman, inventor, businessman, philosopher, and humanitarian.

7

Franklin's father, a poor Boston candlemaker, hoped to make Benjamin, one of 17 children, a minister. But lack of funds forced young Franklin to leave school at the age of 10. Apprenticed to an older brother, a printer, Benjamin managed to educate himself by giving up meat and using the money saved to buy books. Young Benjamin not only educated himself in such basic subjects as arithmetic and English grammar, but also navigation, algebra, geometry, and philosophy.

In 1723, at the age of 17, Ben left Boston to try his luck in Philadelphia. He arrived in that colonial town with little money and no friends. Yet within a very few years, Franklin became a famous author and publisher. His sharp wit and common-sense advice, published in his *Pennsylvania Gazette* and *Poor Richard's Almanack,* were known throughout the American colonies.

Marked up to his credit is a series of diverse achievements never equaled in American history. Here are just a few of his accomplishments:

As a scientist and inventor, Franklin:

1. Proved that lightning consisted of electricity.
2. Invented the lightning rod.
3. Invented the Franklin stove, an economical and useful heating device.
4. Invented bifocal glasses.
5. Invented the platform rocking chair.
6. Wrote a scientific essay which for the first time described the existence of the Gulf Stream.
7. Discovered that poorly aired rooms spread disease.

In the realm of literature, Franklin:

1. Was an original and highly talented writer, whose *Poor Richard's Almanack* and *Autobiography* have assumed a permanent place in the American literary heritage.
2. Founded a popular publication, the *Pennsylvania Gazette,* later to become *The Saturday Evening Post.*

As a humanitarian and tireless contributor to the public welfare, Franklin:

1. Organized the first fire department in Philadelphia.
2. Helped establish the first hospital in America.
3. Founded the first lending library in America.
4. Created the first efficient postal system in America.

5. Founded an academy which later became the University of Pennsylvania.
6. Headed the first society in America to oppose slavery.
7. Established the first American fire insurance company.
8. Founded a club that later became the American Philosophical Society.

Though his accomplishments in any of these fields would have assured Franklin a lasting imprint on American history, it was his role in founding a new nation that gave Franklin his special place in the hearts of his countrymen. Although he had already attained the advanced age of 70 when the Revolutionary War broke out in 1776, Franklin's guiding hand was felt everywhere during the struggle against the British. As Postmaster General of the colonies in rebellion, he contributed his entire salary to help the American wounded. Franklin also took a major part in reorganizing the Continental Army into an efficient fighting force. He helped draft the Declaration of Independence and, as America's envoy to France, did much to forge the alliance that in 1778 brought French aid to the hard-pressed American troops. And it was Franklin's wisdom and gift for compromise that, once the Revolution was won, helped the colonies become a united nation under a federal constitution.

A year before Franklin's death, George Washington wrote the following words to this universally admired American. "If to be venerated for benevolence, if to be admired for talent, if to be esteemed for patriotism, if to be beloved for philanthropy, can gratify the human mind, you must have the pleasing consolation to know you have not lived in vain."

The opossum faints when frightened

When threatened by an enemy, some animals will stand their ground and fight, others will turn tail and run. The opossum, a small American marsupial, prefers another tack: When in danger, the opossum goes into a faint and plays dead!

Once this timid fellow has passed out, his body becomes as rigid as steel. A perplexed predator can poke him, pick him up, roll him over—and still the opossum will remain utterly motionless. Most predators will not eat an animal they have not killed themselves, and, after a few exploratory jabs, will move on to seek other prey. After perhaps twenty minutes of immobility, the opossum will open one eye, glance around to make sure all is well, then climb lazily to his feet and amble off.

Of course, the opossum's sham is not always successful, and many of these helpless creatures never live to awaken from their feigned slumber. But the possum population is certainly in no danger of extinction, for these cowardly creatures are the most prolific mammals in existence. An opossum may bear three litters in a single year—with as many as eighteen babies in each litter!

Marcgravia flowers are natural Christmas tree ornaments

For sheer visual peculiarity, nature has produced few plants more remarkable than the marcgravia. The flower clusters of this South American forest dweller dangle from their stalks like delicate Christmas tree ornaments. The flowers suspended from the clusters resemble tiny mobiles. But this fanciful structure is far from accidental, for the marcgravia—like almost all flowers—is expressly designed to facilitate its pollination.

Each flower cluster consists of five nectar pouches and a number of much smaller flowers. The pipe-shaped pouches hang vertically, with the acorn-shaped flowers suspended above in a horizontal whorl. Hummingbirds which visit the pouches to extract nectar cannot avoid bumping the flowers as they leave. Pollen is thus left on the birds' heads, and deposited on the flowers they subsequently visit, thereby pollinating those plants.

The marcgravia is notable also for the unusual formation of its leaves. The lower portion of each stem produces two rows of stalkless leaves. But higher up, near the flower, the leaves are stalked and arranged spirally around the stem. The change from one arrangement to the other is abrupt—and its cause unknown.

The ostrich can outrun a racehorse

The ostrich is the largest bird in the world, standing about eight feet tall and weighing up to three hundred pounds. A bird this size can't fly, of course, but the ostrich is certainly no slowpoke on land. A running ostrich can cover twenty-five feet in one stride, and at top speed can reach almost sixty miles an hour—faster than many racehorses!

According to popular belief, an endangered ostrich will bury his head in the sand. Actually, the bird is capable of outrunning almost any enemy. And even if he is cornered unexpectedly, this swift creature is far from defenseless—one kick of his powerful legs can kill a man!

In some parts of the world ostriches are raised for their feathers. Gauchos in the Argentine Pampas use bolas to bring down the big birds.

**The trunk of the baobab is large enough
to house a family**

"The devil plucked up the baobab, thrust its branches into the earth, and left its roots in the air." To the Arabs who developed this legend, there seemed perhaps no other way to explain the preposterous shape of the baobab tree, an African and Indian relative of the cacao. With its broad, bulging trunk and dense network of root-like branches, the baobab does indeed appear to have been thrust upside down into the earth.

The trunks of these giants—second in bulk only to the sequoias—are extraordinarily fat in relation to their height. While the average baobab is only about 45 feet high, its diameter often approaches 35 feet, and some specimens are actually broader than they are tall!

The pulpy inside of this trunk is so soft that a bullet could pass right through it. African natives take advantage of the tree's softness and girth by hollowing out the trunk and using it as a dwelling. One famous South African specimen has been hollowed out and used as a bus shelter!

In addition to its unique shape, the baobab can boast one of the most extensive root systems in nature. The horizontal roots of some specimens spread out as much as 300 feet around the plant.

Daniel Dancer was the world's worst miser

In the annals of miserdom, no account is more pitiable than that of Daniel Dancer and his sister, who lived and died in 18th-century England. Daniel, however, was the stingier of the two, for in the worship of Mammon, he sacrificed his sister's life.

Lying on the heap of rags that was her bed, the dying Miss Dancer worsened from day to day, yet received no medical attention. When asked why he did not call a doctor for his sister, Daniel replied, "Why should I waste my money in wickedly endeavoring to counteract the will of Providence?"

All the while his sister lay ill, Daniel made no change in her customary diet of one cold dumpling and a strip of fatty meat. When she objected that so meager a supper would not suffice for one who was sick, Daniel told her, "If you don't like it, you may go without it."

The Dancer siblings were by no means poor: they had an annual income of 3,000 pounds a year from their farmlands in Harrow, just south of London. Yet they were so frugal that on one occasion, while walking on their grounds, they came upon the rotting carcass of a sheep that had obviously died of disease. They skinned this decaying hulk, and made meat pies with what little flesh remained.

Daniel Dancer would obtain fertilizer for his fields by walking along the common road, stuffing his pockets with the cow dung he found there. While he had his nose to the ground for manure, he also foraged for old bones; what meat was on the bones would go toward his dinner, while the bone would go to his dog.

From time to time, the Dancers received the charity of one Lady Tempest. On a frigid winter night, she sent Daniel a trout stewed in claret. During transport, the trout froze. Dancer was faced with a formidable challenge: he would not eat the trout cold, for fear of contracting a toothache; yet he would not warm the fish on a fire, not wanting to expend the wood. So in a miserly stroke of genius, he sat on his dinner like a hen until the delicacy thawed.

⬥

The Kaufmann house at Bear Run, Pennsylvania, is built directly over a waterfall

"Fallingwater" is the popular name for one of the best-known private residences in the country, the Edgar J. Kaufmann house on Bear Run, Pennsylvania. The name is appropriate, for this home—designed by America's premier architect, Frank Lloyd Wright—was built directly over a waterfall!

When Mr. Kaufmann commissioned Wright to design a week-end retreat for his family on his Pennsylvania property, he wanted the architect to take full advantage of the picturesque site: a wooden glen with a slowly running stream, a clear pool, and a small waterfall. And Wright more than fulfilled his expectations, designing a striking three-story structure anchored on a small cliff overlooking the pool, with a portion of the house cantilevered directly over the running water.

Built almost entirely of masonry, the home features six reinforced-concrete terraces extending over the waterfall and pool. Most rooms offer access to a terrace and a breathtaking vista of the waters below. A stairway suspended from the lower story reaches to within a few feet of the waterfall itself. Viewed from the pool, Fallingwater seems to rise from the boulders around it, and

the stream appears to run directly through the house, as if the structure were part of the natural site rather than an addition to it.

The unusual site and construction of Fallingwater earned the home much publicity when it was completed in 1936, and the home remains one of Wright's best-loved works. Fallingwater is open to visitors.

Thirty people can stand in the observation deck at the crown of the Statue of Liberty

Towering above the harbor of New York, the gateway to America, the Statue of Liberty has stood as a welcoming beacon to millions of immigrants and visitors for close to 100 years.

What a thrill it is, after a long voyage, to slip through the Narrows Channel into the Upper Bay and suddenly view the vast panorama of New York City, with the great lady standing tall in the midst of the busy harbor, facing the open sea, her torch held high above her head in welcome.

18

The full name of this world-famous monument is The Statue of Liberty Enlightening the World. As befitting a monument to universal liberty, the Statue was erected not by any monarch or government, but the citizens of France and the United States, the twin vanguard of democracy.

An organization known as the Franco-American Union was founded in 1875, the year before America's centennial celebration. A proposal by the Frenchman Edouard Laboulayé was adopted whereby donations from American and French citizens would be used for the design and construction of a monument to commemorate the American and French Revolutions, and to symbolize the long-standing friendship between these two nations.

French citizens raised money for the statue, and a design was accepted from Frederic Auguste Bartholdi for an iron-and-steel frame statue covered with copper sheets. American citizens raised the money for the granite-and-concrete pedestal. Bartholdi, during a visit to the United States, suggested that the statue be placed on 12-acre Bedloe's Island, in the middle of New York Harbor.

American builders constructed the pedestal atop an 11-point star formed by the walls of old Fort Wood, which had previously occupied the island. Rising atop the pedestal was the iron-and-steel frame designed by Charles Eiffel—who was later to build the Eiffel Tower. When the 300 sculptured copper sheets were fixed to the frame, the copper-colored colossus was left towering above the bay. (Copper oxidizes with age, and today the statue is entirely green.)

The Statue of Liberty was dedicated on October 28, 1886, and in 1924, it became a National Monument. In 1960, the name of Bedloe's Island was officially changed to Liberty Island.

The statue itself is a 152-foot figure of a woman in long robes, raising a lighted torch above her head. In her left hand she holds a tablet on which the date July 4, 1776—the date of the signing of the Declaration of Independence—is inscribed. Around her feet lie broken chains, symbolic of the breaking of the bonds of oppression that the statue commemorates. The pedestal adds nearly another 150 feet, giving the monument a total height of over 300 feet.

Visitors can take an elevator to the top of the pedestal, then climb a narrow, winding staircase that twists up into the Lady's crown. There, an observation room 260 feet above the water affords up to 30 people a spectacular view of New York harbor. In earlier days, visitors were permitted to climb to the arm of the statue and emerge on a platform surrounding the torch, but this passageway has been closed off in recent years, due to suspected structural weaknesses in the arm.

Whether one views the city from atop the statue or admires the statue from the city and harbor below, the Statue of Liberty remains an inspiring monument, a structural wonder, and the symbol of a nation.

⧯⧯⧯

A seed of the Seychelles coconut can outweigh a bushel of apples

When you think of a seed, you're likely to call to mind an apple or melon seed, or an orange or cherry pit, all of which are roughly the same size. But just as plants themselves vary greatly in their dimensions, so do their seeds. Certain orchids produce seeds so small that 35 million would weigh just an ounce. At the other end of the scale, the seed of the Seychelles coconut can weigh more than a bushel of apples!

The Seychelles coconut is a palm tree found only in the Seychelles, a group of small islands off the east coast of Africa. It is often called the double coconut, because the shape of its seeds resemble two coconuts joined together. The seeds also bear a remarkable resemblance to the female pelvis, and as a result, magical properties have traditionally been attributed to the plant. The palm is sometimes known by yet another name, *coco de mer* (coconut of the sea), for its seeds have floated around the world and washed up on many distant shores.

Technically, the "seed" of this rare palm is a fruit, for it consists of a fleshy, fibrous jacket surrounding a hard, two-lobed seed. But since each fruit contains only one seed, many naturalists consider the Seychelles' fruit as a seed—indeed, as the largest seed in the world. (In fact, the largest true seed is that of the South American *Mora* tree, which can grow as long as six inches.)

The giant "seed" of the Seychelles coconut takes up to 10 years to ripen, sometimes attaining a length of 18 inches and a weight of 40 or 50 pounds!

**Cote covered ten miles on snowshoes in a
little over an hour**

Gerard Cote was an athlete for all seasons. In warm weather, he
was a distance runner who had won the famous 26-mile Boston
Marathon three times. In winter, he was a snowshoer.

One fine day in 1938, the French Canadian ventured down to
Montreal from his home in St. Hyacinthe for the national champi-

onships. Wearing standard 10" by 33" snowshoes, the 24-year-old newsboy, who stood only five feet, six inches tall and weighed a mere 130 pounds, clomped over the 10-mile course in 63 minutes and 45 seconds—a record performance.

Edgerton won a professional fight at age 63

When ex-boxer Walter Edgerton, age 63, challenged ex-boxer John Henry Johnson to a fight, Edgerton was at an age when most men would prefer to be puttering in their gardens. Johnson was no kid, either—he was 45.

Back in the 1880's Edgerton had been a well-known feather-weight—"Kentucky Rosebud" by name. But this was February, 1913, and his fighting days should have been long behind him.

One fine day at a bar, Edgerton got into an argument with another ex-boxer. Herman Taylor, a young promoter, heard about the quarrel and understood that the two wanted to settle their falling out with their fists. The age factor didn't faze them at all. So Taylor suggested they go into the ring at the Broadway AC. Not only would they end their altercation in the time-honored manner, but they would pick up some prize money as well.

And they did. The night Edgerton and Johnson squared off, the little AC was packed to its 800 capacity.

When he entered the ring at Philadelphia's Broadway Athletic Club, Edgerton didn't show an overabundance of push and go. At the start, it wasn't the fastest-moving bout on record. But Edgerton was conserving his strength. Before the fourth round was over, the young John Henry, Edgerton's junior by 18 years, was laid out like a plank, felled by the "Rosebud's" knockout punch.

Baby Clark was born without a brain

On May 26, 1788, a 26-year-old woman named Mary Clark gave birth in the Carlisle Dispensary, England. The child was perfectly developed, except for a somewhat soft head. The doctor passed this off, since the child cried, kicked, ate, and otherwise behaved quite normally; moreover, a baby's head is normally rather soft.

After five days, inexplicably, the tot died. An autopsy revealed the startling fact that the child's skull contained neither a cerebrum, nor a cerebellum, nor a medulla—in short, *no brain.*

Incredible as the case may seem, it is not the only instance of a human being living without a brain. In 1935, another such child was born in St. Vincent's Hospital in New York City. Just like the Clark child, this babe acted normally for all the days of its life—27.

The cause of death was unknown until an autopsy revealed that the infant's head contained nothing but water.

William Beckford was England's mad builder of towers

William Beckford was but a child when he inherited his father's West Indies plantation, a million pounds, and a sumptuous estate in Wiltshire, England. His guardian saw to it that he obtained the finest education possible. On the Continent, he learned piano from Mozart, and Arabic and Persian from private tutors.

In 1786, at the age of 26, Beckford wrote an Arabian romance called *Vathek* which was greatly admired by Byron, and is still studied in universities today. For some unknown reason, the Englishman Beckford wrote his book in French, *and then hired someone to translate it into English,* the language in which it was first published.

In Beckford's novel, an Arabian sultan named Vathek builds an enormous tower, hoping to fathom the secrets of the universe through a study of astrology. In the 1790's, the sultan's preoccupation in the novel became Beckford's preoccupation in reality. Beckford hired England's greatest architect of the time, James Wyatt, to build him a tower as magnificent as Vathek's.

Beckford was terribly impatient for Fonthill Abbey, as he named the structure, to be completed. He had 500 men working on the job night and day, in two shifts. He pressed the workers so hard that they were compelled to take many structural shortcuts.

In 1800, the 300-foot tower was completed. Beckford prepared to move in. But not one week after the tower was completed, the first mild zephyr broke it in half, and reduced the structure to rubble.

Beckford went to work again, this time determined that his tower would *not* fall. He invested seven years and 273,000 pounds to erect it. For 15 years, Beckford lived in this 300-foot tower, until financial reverses forced him to sell it to a man named John Farquhar. Not long after Farquhar moved in, the tower collapsed in a gale.

Beckford's next and last construction was the maddest of his career. On a hill outside the resort town of Bath, Beckford built a modest tower of 130 feet, and stocked it with dwarfs. By now, the middle-aged Beckford had acquired a considerable aversion to women, which he formalized in stone. He had special niches constructed in the hallways, so that his maids could hide themselves when they heard his approach.

Poon Lim survived for 133 days on a life raft

On November 23, 1942, the S.S. Lomond, an English merchant manned by a crew of 55, was torpedoed in the South Atlantic. Only one of the seamen survived—a 25-year-old Chinese by the name of Poon Lim. He had been catapulted off the deck by an explosion of such force that the very clothes were blown from his back.

Lim swam in the neighborhood of the wreck for two hours, and then grabbed a drifting life raft on which he survived for 133 days, naked and exposed to the elements. The raft carried enough food

and water for him to live through 60 days. After that, his very life depended on the fish he could catch.

Poon fashioned a hook from a spring which he extracted from the raft's flashlight, and he trolled for small fish. He used these small ones as bait for larger game. Occasionally, he would grab at and catch a sea gull for a meatier meal.

But hunger was not his only trial. Verily, Poon Lim was like Coleridge's "ancient mariner," who bemoaned:

> *Alone, alone, oh! all alone,*
> *Alone on a wide, wide sea;*
> *And never a saint took pity on*
> *My soul in agony.*

For more than four months, Lim drifted through calm and squall, and at long last neared the coast of Brazil. On April 5, 1943, he was spotted by some fishermen who took him aboard. He was palpably ill, and his legs were wobbly, but yet his rescuers found it hard to believe that this 5-foot, 5-inch little mite of a man could have possibly endured through better than a third of a year on an exposed raft, bobbing at random in the middle of the ocean.

When the story reached Britain the tale met with a different reception. The British knew about the torpedoing of the S.S. Lomond. King George VI, deeply impressed with Poon's fortitude, presented him in 1943 with England's highest civilian award, the British Empire medal. Speaking of his incredible record, Poon Lim said, "I hope no one will ever have to break it."

Salo Finkelstein was a mathematical machine

Some few years before World War II, the Polish Treasury Department began an economy drive by hiring Salo Finkelstein of Warsaw. Dr. Finkelstein merely replaced some 40-odd people, each of whom had operated a calculating machine. And the Polish Government vouched for the fact that during the five years in which

Dr. Finkelstein tossed huge columns of figures around in his head, he did not make a mistake.

For Salo Finkelstein was a genius if ever there was one. You could give him a large number like 3,108, and in less than one minute he would reduce it accurately to the following squares: 52^2, 16^2, 12^2, and 2^2—a simple little maneuver that would take most of us half an hour or more to work out, if we could do it at all. The Doctor could look at an arithmetical problem like 6,894 x 2,763, and in just seven seconds, without paper and pencil, come up with the answer.

In his public performances, Finkelstein did use a blackboard. He drew a square containing five rows of five spaces, or 25 spaces in all. Then he turned his back to the board.

Folks in the audience came up and filled in the spaces with numbers. Finkelstein turned around and took one quick glance at the blackboard. Then, either blindfolded or with his back turned to the board, he recited the 25 numbers, going from left to right, then going from top to bottom, then moving diagonally, then spirally; or in fact, in any way that you might ask him to juggle his figures. And an hour later, after his mind had been filled with every conceivable sort of calculation, he would repeat those 25 numbers.

You see, the numbers were engraved on that photographic mind of his just as if they had been impressed on a gelatin plate. He remembered pi to 300 decimal places. He could recite logarithms from 1 to 100 to the seventh decimal and from 101 to 150 to the fifth decimal. He could conjure up, without a second's hesitation, thousands of square roots, cube roots, products, quotients, and number combinations. These numbers never failed him. They were there in his mind, and they stuck!

The 300-year-old secret of Stradivarius remains unsolved

Antonius Stradivarius was born in 1644. Initially a woodcarver, he learned to play the violin and consequently became interested in the making of violins. At eighteen he became an apprentice to Niccolo Amati, the famous violinmaker of Cremona.

In 1680, he left Amati's shop and began to work for himself. He experimented with his violins, giving them many different shapes. He was obsessed with the desire to make his violin sound as lovely as a beautiful human voice. He decorated his violins so exquisitely—inlaying them with mother of pearl and ivory and ebony—that not only are they the world's most wonderful violins because of their exquisite tone, but they are also the most beautiful violins ever created.

By the time he was 40 years old, he was a renowned and extremely wealthy man. He kept his notes safely locked up. Not even his two sons, who labored with him in his workshop, knew his secrets. During his long life of 94 years, he made at least 1,116 instruments.

The hunt for the secret of Stradivarius has been carried on ever since his death in 1737. His violins have been carefully measured and copied in every detail, and some very fine violins have been made; but they have never attained the perfection of the master's instruments. Vuillane, a famous French violinmaker of the early 1800's, spent all his life searching for the secrets of the great Stradivarius. At last, he finally got in touch with Giacomo Stradivarius, the great grandson of the master. Giacomo told Vuillane that he had discovered in an old family Bible a formula for varnish which he believed to have been Antonius Stradivarius' own special formula. Giacomo said he had told no one about it and, even though he was sorely tempted during financial straits to sell it, he had made the decision that he would give nobody the priceless prescription except a member of the family, should any one of them decide to pursue the trade of violinmaker.

Diverse suppositions have been made about what makes the violins of Stradivarius supreme. Some have attributed the characteristic sound of his violins to the physical properties of the wood, or to the shape of the instruments; others maintain that the secret lay in the interrelation of the various parts of the instruments. Still others regard the answer as the special pitch which Stradivarius derived from the sap of trees then growing in Italy which have since disappeared. But the most widely believed theory is that Stradivarius' secret lies in the special composition of the varnish with which he coated his violins. Chemists have attempted to analyze the composition, and indeed, some violinmakers have greatly improved the tone of their violins by imitating as closely as possible the composition of Stradivarius' varnish. Nevertheless, no one has been able to discover his secret. It is as much a mystery today as it was nearly 250 years ago.

Rollings did 17,000 consecutive sit-ups

Sit-ups are a standard form of exercise used in many calisthenics classes. To do a sit-up, one lies on one's back with hands folded behind the head. The idea is to keep the legs stretched flat on the floor and then to raise the rest of the body up, bending the trunk at the waist until the elbows touch the knees. Generally speaking, 20 or at the most 30 of such sit-ups are all the average man or woman can perform. An individual who has been honed to especially good condition may do 100 sit-ups.

On September 13, 1971, Wayne E. Rollings, a 30-year-old Marine captain stationed at Kaneohe, Hawaii, summoned official witnesses and medical aides to the gymnasium of his military post to authenticate his feat.

Wayne began doing sit-ups, and didn't stop until he had done a total of 17,000, achieving this number in 7 hours 27 minutes.

Gama, a 5-foot 7-inch Indian, was the greatest wrestler in history

Although much smaller than most wrestlers you see on TV, Gama of Patiala, India, made up for his size, and then some. Generally acknowledged to be the top wrestler of all time, this 5-foot 7-inch, 260-pound battler had a hard time finding competition. Most wrestlers feared Gama so much they would not enter the ring with him. Gama reigned as world champ well into his fifties.

In London in 1910, the Indian challenged any 20 wrestlers to meet him in combat, promising to throw them all in succession within an hour. But the Britons wouldn't take on the Indian terror. Indeed, throughout his career, Gama was able to lure only two Occidentals to do battle with him. One was an American named B.F. Roller; the other a Pole, the world-famous professional wrestler Stanislaus Zbysko, a gigantic hunk of a man, and generally regarded by sports writers as a very competent athlete. Neither lasted more than half a minute.

The narwhal's tusk is often half as long as its body

The narwhal is a large aquatic mammal that makes its home in the coastal waters of the Arctic Ocean. This curious-looking creature has only two teeth in its upper jaw, and in the male of the species, one of these teeth develops into a long, straight tusk—giving him the appearance of a seal with a spearlike horn projecting straight ahead. Although the narwhal averages only thirteen or fourteen feet in length, occasionally growing to twenty feet, narwhal tusks are sometimes nine feet long—almost half as long as the creature's body!

The function of this oversized tusk is not known. The narwhal uses it neither as a digging tool nor as a weapon in combat. But during the Middle Ages this ivory spear was highly prized by man as the fabled horn of the unicorn.

Blake surf rode a wave for almost a mile

In popular fancy, good surfers are imagined capable of riding a wave for several miles. This is a misconception, for even at Honolulu's Waikiki Beach, generally considered to offer the finest surfing conditions in the world, the average ride is no more than 200 yards. Occasionally, though, when surf and tide conditions are right, longer rides become possible—at least for the best surfers, *if* they are lucky enough to be in the right place at the right time.

33

Commonplace 200-yard rides take place at Waikiki when the surf is running at "blow-hole-break," which is just about every day. (A break is a point where a wave slows, builds up, and then scatters.) At "first-break," which occurs somewhat less often, a good surfer can make 300 yards. When the surf breaks at Kalahuewehe, or "castle-break," he can make 500 yards, but this condition occurs only about three times a year. Even less frequent is "chuna-break," a condition when half-mile rides are possible. The longest rides of all occur when the surf comes in at "zero-break," something that very rarely happens.

It did happen, though, just before sundown one evening early in June 1936, and Tom Blake, probably the top surfer of all time, was on the spot and ready. In fact, Tom had been ready and waiting for a chance like this for six years.

The tide was running extremely high off Waikiki that day, so Blake knew something big was coming; though, of course, he had no way of predicting that it would be "zero-break." Along with several other skilled surfers, he took to the water and calmly edged his board into position far out at the mouth of Waikiki Bay.

Watching intently, Blake suddenly observed a set of monster waves rearing up about a half-mile off. Here, indeed, was the big one!

Catching the second wave of the set, Blake began riding in toward the beach atop a 25-foot-high solid wall of water stretching across the full width of Waikiki Bay. None of his companions made it, but Blake, progressing rapidly from "first-break-south-castle" through "public-baths break" and "chuna-break," soon reached the shore opposite Lalani Village. He had completed a surf ride of about a mile, the longest ever recorded.

Rastelli juggled 10 balls

Enrico Rastelli was one of the greatest jugglers and acrobats of all time. A magnificently coordinated athlete, he had the highest paid novelty act of any kind when he worked the Keith Albee-Orpheum vaudeville circuit in the United States in the 1920s.

The son and grandson of performers, Rastelli was born in 1896 in Samara, Russia, where his parents were on tour with the famous Circus Truzzi. He learned juggling from his father, and at the age of 12, he displayed his budding talent by doing a handstand on his father's head while juggling four lit torches.

The wiry 5-foot 6-inch Rastelli soon gained fame for many incredible feats. He would do a handstand on a lamp which stood on a table, while he was also holding an 8-foot flagpole (which flew the Italian flag) with one foot, and juggling two balls with his other foot. Rastelli could also juggle six 24-inch sticks while keeping a seventh stick balanced on his head, and he could juggle eight plates at one time.

However, his most famous stunt was the one in which he flashed ten balls at one time—that is, simultaneously kept five balls constantly moving with each hand. No juggler since has been able to duplicate this feat.

Bats fly by radar

As the expression "blind as a bat" indicates, bats have extremely poor vision. Yet these creatures—the only flying mammals in existence—can navigate easily in the blackest night, gobbling up insects that would be invisible to the sharpest human eye. How do they do it? Surprisingly enough, bats fly by radar!

When a ship is negotiating a difficult strait in fog or darkness, it sends out radio signals that strike nearby objects and bounce back to the ship. The time it takes for these signals to reach the object and return to the ship indicates how far away that object is.

The bat's "radar" system works on the same principle. As he

flies through the air, the bat opens his mouth and sends out a steady series of rapid little cries, from thirty to sixty per second. These cries are much too high-pitched to be detected by human ears, but the bat can hear sounds pitched as high as 100,000 vibrations per second. If the sounds strike an object, they bounce back, like an echo. The bat's remarkable ears pick them up and tell him where the object is located.

The radar system of this airborne creature is so precise that a totally blind bat can fly about in a crowded room wthout touching an obstacle with so much as a wing tip. But tape his mouth shut and he'll crash into everything—including the wall!

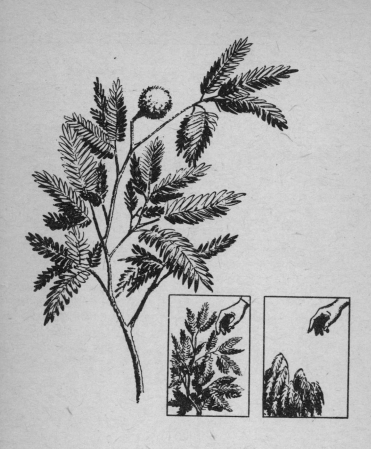

The "sensitive plant" droops immediately if stimulated

One of the most remarkable examples of a plant's ability to react to external stimuli is the movement exhibited by a plant known as *Mimosa pudica*. So strong are the reactive properties of this species of mimosa that it is commonly termed the "sensitive plant." If you were to perform some simple experiments, you might believe that this plant is capable of experiencing both fright and fatigue!

When flourishing, the long, thin leaves of the sensitive plant extend straight outward from their stem in symmetrical pairs, with the stem itself erect. But when one of the leaves is touched, all the leaves immediately raise themselves vertically and fold over until each pair has joined together near the stem. The stem then bends downward limply. These drooping movements, which take just seconds, give the impression that the entire plant is wilting from fright before your very eyes!

The mimosa will react to strong wind, warmth, vibration, sudden darkness, and other stimuli as well as touch. After a short time in the wilted, closed-up condition, the leaves will begin spreading slowly until they have returned to their normal position. But another touch can send them drooping again.

Curiously, a sensitive plant can be overstimulated. If the plant is touched repeatedly within a short period of time, it will cease to react after a few openings and closings—as if it had become exhausted by its movements! Moreover, in certain temperature ranges the mimosa will not react at all.

These unusual movements are due to small cushion-like bodies, called pulvini, found at the base of the leaf stalks. When the leaves are extended, the pulvini are firm and filled with water. When the plant is stimulated, an electrical impulse is transmitted throughout the plant, and the water quickly passes out of the pulvini and into the stem. The deflated pulvini can no longer buoy up the leaves, and the plant wilts with "fright."

A 20-pound porcupine can kill a 200-pound lion

If you've ever stumbled into a cactus plant, you know what it would be like to trip over a porcupine in the dark. This odd creature has hundreds of treacherous quills protruding from his back, sides, and tail, providing him with one of nature's most unusual—and most successful—defense mechanisms.

Many people erroneously believe that the porcupine shoots his quills like darts. Actually, the quills are very loose and come off at the slightest touch, so that in a fight it may appear that the por-

cupine is shooting them. Nevertheless, this thorny fellow—who is no bigger than a large tomcat—is capable of killing a beast as huge as a mountain lion!

Ordinarily lions—as well as bears, wolves, and other woodland predators—wisely keep their distance from this walking pincushion. But occasionally a hungry cat will leap on a porcupine. When attacked, the slow-footed rodent merely turns his back. After one bite the foolhardy cat's mouth is bristling with sharp quills.

The tip of each quill is barbed like a fish hook, and the more the lion struggles to spit out the unwelcome lunch, the deeper the quills sink into the tender lining of his mouth. Swallowing only breaks off the ends of the quills and pierces the membrane of his throat. In a few days the lion, unable to eat, will die of starvation.

There's only one animal clever enough to overcome the porcupine—the fisher, a member of the weasel family. The fisher walks quietly up to the porcupine and, instead of scratching or biting, merely turns the spiny beast over on his back and slits his soft belly with his claws.

The porcupine's own diet consists mostly of the juicy underbark of trees. Occasionally, though, a porcupine will lumber into a campsite in search of his favorite dish—salt.

The porcupine's love of salt is nothing short of phenomenal. He will even lick the wood on porch steps if people have walked barefoot on the boards, for there is enough salt in human sweat to send the porcupine into gustatory ecstasy. And if you've wondered why deer antlers are so hard to find in the woods, blame it on the porcupine's passion for salt. The thorny rodents chew the horns up and swallow them for their salty flavor!

Mathias won the Olympic decathlon at age 17

No title is held in greater esteem than the Olympic decathlon. The champion in this event is generally regarded as the greatest athlete in the world. There is no doubt that the performances in the 1968 decathlon in Mexico City were watched on television by more viewers than any other Olympic event. The decathlon performer must be able to run, to jump, and to throw. He must be able to sprint, and to have sufficient endurance to last a long distance. He must blend agility with strength.

Just a few months before he was tapped to carry the hopes of the United States in the 1948 Olympics in London, 17-year-old Bob Mathias had never touched a javelin. Nor had he ever pole-vaulted. And to top off his inexperience, the 400-meter distance and the 1,500-meter distance were quite unfamiliar. His enthusiastic high school coach suggested to his young charge that he try out for the Olympic team anyhow. The lad weighed 190 pounds, was strong, willing, and was an exceptionally good competitor. Bob Mathias was the cool type. The coach believed that he wouldn't make the team, but that he would gain valuable experience for the next competition, four years later.

However, Mathias exceeded everyone's hopes, including his own. He won the very first decathlon meet he entered, defeating several well-known college stars. Less than a month later, he won the U.S. championship. In a short six weeks, the boy found himself in the international arena in London.

Here Mathias took on the world's best as if he were a veteran. The schoolboy ran the 100 meters in 11.2 seconds; the 400 meters in 51.7 seconds; the rugged 1,500 meters in 5 minutes and 11 seconds; the 110-meter hurdles in 15.7 seconds. He broad-jumped 21 feet 8 inches; high-jumped 6 feet 1¼ inches, and pole-vaulted 11

feet 5½ inches. In the weight events, he threw the javelin 165 feet 1 inch; the shot put, 42 feet 9 inches; and he hurled the discus 144 feet 4 inches. His 7,139 points easily led the field.

When the two-day ordeal ended on August 6, an onlooker asked Bob what he would do to celebrate his victory. "Start shaving, I guess," said Bob.

The sloth's belly is almost constantly filled

The title of "the laziest animal in the world" must go to a small, tropical American mammal known as the sloth—his very name means "slow"! This sluggish creature spends almost his entire life clinging erect to the trunk of a tree or hanging upside down from a branch. He doesn't make a single move unless it's absolutely necessary!

The sloth is a queer-looking fellow with a rounded head and a grotesque, flattened face. One species of sloth has two toes on his forelegs; another species—also known as the ai—has three toes. Both species have sharp, curved claws for clinging to trees, and both species are equally lazy—but with good reason. For the sloth cannot walk—if he ever moves along the ground he does so by pulling his body along with his claws. And his belly is almost constantly filled! It may take a sloth more than a week to digest a meal, and in the meantime, he does nothing but hang motionless from a branch.

Despite his sluggishness, the sloth has little to fear from other creatures of the jungle. Suspended from a branch, this little loafer resembles a clump of dead leaves, and during the rainy season he derives additional camouflage from a green alga that grows in his hair. And should some rude creature on the ground below disturb a slumbering sloth, the lazy fellow can investigate the noise-maker with a minimum of effort—due to an unusual arrangement of neck vertebrae, a sloth can turn his head through a 270-degree angle!

Bangkok contains 400 Buddhist temples

Bangkok, Thailand, is the home of some of the most stunning Buddhist monasteries within the limits of this canal-crossed city, often called the "Venice of the East."

Perhaps the most well-known of Bangkok's many religious structures is the Temple of the Emerald Buddha. Since the 15th century, when King Tiloka adopted the structure as the spiritual safeguard of Thailand, the Temple of the Emerald Buddha has

44

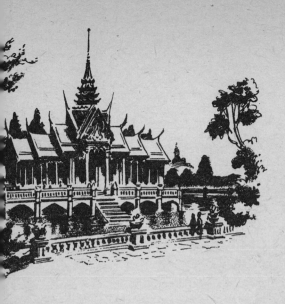

been the center of all Thai religious life. The Temple is the home of the most sacred objects in Thailand, chief among these an immense statue of a meditating Buddha mounted on a pedestal under the Temple's high roof.

The Emerald Buddha forms only a part of a larger religious complex, called the Wat Phra Kaeo, situated on the banks of the Chaophraya River in the Thai capital. The complex is surrounded by a wall four and one-half miles long, 13 feet high, and 10 feet thick. Sixty-three ornamented gates permit entry to the sacred grounds.

In addition to the Emerald Buddha, the Wat Phra Kaeo includes a depository of ancient Buddhist scriptures, memorials to white elephants, statues of venerated holy men, and a great stupa or reliquary. The Royal Pantheon—which is open to visitors only one day each year—contains life-sized bronze figures of former Thai kings. Throughout the grounds, tall plaster demons, or Yaks, have been placed to ward off evil spirits.

In every building of the temple complex, each door, window,

statue, tower, and pillar tapers upwards. The most striking features of these buildings are the "sky licks," curving, pointed pieces of ornamental metal that resembles licks of flame.

Directly across the Chaophraya River from Wat Phra Kaeo lies the small Wat Arun, or Temple of the Dawn. Here, as in the Wat Phra Kaeo, the brick walls are intricately inlaid with bits of shell, pottery, and porcelain. The various levels of the Wat Arun are supported by rows of columns sculpted in the form of demons.

The two temple complexes, bordering the river with their needlepoint towers glittering in the sun, form one of the most memorable panoramas in the East—or for that matter, in the world.

Pheidippides ran from Marathon to Athens

In September of 490 B.C., King Darius, the ruler of the powerful Persian Empire, sent his army to attack the city-state of Athens. His forces landed on the plain of Marathon, just a few miles from Athens.

Though greatly outnumbered, the Athenians marched out to meet the invaders, while sending a request for help to their allies in Sparta. The message was carried by Pheidippides, the best runner in Athens.

Racing out of the city on foot, he ran all that day and through the night, forging ahead across rough, rocky terrain in which the road was often barely suitable for mules and mountain goats. The next morning, having covered a distance of 140 miles, he arrived in Sparta. After delivering his message and getting the answer, he set out to rejoin the Athenian troops, once again covering the distance in a day and a night.

Just a few days later, the Athenian and Persian armies clashed in the now famous battle of Marathon. Though he'd had only a short time to rest up from his magnificent two-way run, Pheidippides participated in the battle as an infantryman.

Contrary to expectations, the Athenians decisively defeated the Persians. Like his fellow soldiers, who had fought so hard against the numerically superior enemy, Pheidippides was exhausted when the fighting came to an end. Nonetheless, he gamely accept-

ed the Athenian commander's request to carry the news of the victory to the anxious inhabitants of the city. Casting off his heavy armor, the exhausted Pheidippides set out on his last and greatest run.

The distance from Marathon to Athens is 22 miles 1,470 yards. Pheidippides covered it in just a few hours, but the ordeal was too much for his already overtaxed system. Shouting, "Victory, victory" with his last breaths, he staggered into the central marketplace of Athens, then dropped to the pavement—dead.

The Athenians never forgot this noble patriotic sacrifice; and in the years that followed, they established a series of memorial games, including running events of various kinds, in memory of Pheidippides. When the Olympic Games were revived in 1896, a road-race called the marathon was made a regular event. In 1924, its distance was standardized at 26 miles 385 yards.

The Kremlin is the largest fortress in Europe

Today, Moscow's Kremlin is synonymous with the government of the Soviet Union. But the Kremlin is also a construction of extraordinary beauty and size. In fact, this age-old complex is the largest fortress in all Europe.

In medieval Russia, a kremlin was a walled bastion within a city which provided protection for the rulers who resided there, and served as the administrative and religious center of the surrounding district. A kremlin customarily included palaces, churches, barracks, storehouses, and markets, and hence, was a small city in itself.

The kremlin at Moscow, now known simply as the Kremlin, was the seat of the Czarist government until 1712, when the Rus-

sian capital was moved to St. Petersburg (now Leningrad). In 1918, after the Bolshevik revolution, the capital was relocated in Moscow, and the Kremlin became the center of administration for the Soviet Union.

This massive city-within-a-city was built in stages over a period of six centuries. The first stone structures were erected in 1365, and the Czar Ivan III rebuilt the entire complex a century later. Over the years, the Kremlin has many times survived the destruction of Moscow itself. In 1812, during Napoleon's occupation, the Kremlin alone withstood the inferno that burned almost the entire city to the ground.

The Kremlin is situated on a small hill overlooking the Moscow River. The fortress consists of a complex of varied buildings surrounded by a triangular wall one-and-one-quarter miles around. In all, the Kremlin extends over an area of 90 acres.

49

Many of the structures that comprise the Kremlin are world-famous in themselves. The Palace of Facets, built by Italian architects in the late 15th century, is a charming milk-white palace noted for the diamond-shaped facets that adorn its facades. The Grand Palace, built in the 19th century, is the largest building within the Kremlin, and today houses the Supreme Soviet, the parliament of the Soviet Union.

The Spasskaya Tower, one of the Kremlin's 20 gate towers, is the most famous tower in all Russia. Nearby, the 270-foot Ivan the Great Bell Tower—the highest structure in the Kremlin—rises to a golden onion-shaped dome.

The renowned King of Bells, the largest bell in the world, is on display near the Bell Tower. This gigantic instrument, cast in 1733, weighs 216 tons and is over 20 feet high. Twenty-four men were required to swing its clapper. Unfortunately, the bell fell to the ground after only three years of use, and has not been tolled since.

The Kremlin also contains the largest cannon in the world, a gun so huge it has never been fired.

On the eastern side of the Kremlin lies the famed Red Square, the site of the incredibly beautiful cathedral of St. Basil. This ornate church, built in the later 16th century, is remarkable for its multi-colored onion-shaped domes. Another feature of Red Square is the black marble tomb of Lenin.

The Ziggurat was the emblem of a great ancient culture

The ziggurat form was in common use for pyramidal temples in the ancient kingdoms of Sumer, Babylonia, and Assyria. At one time, hundreds of these huge structures—often called step pyramids—stood in the various kingdoms of Mesopotamia (now Iraq). The Biblical story of the Tower of Babel relates one attempt to build such a temple, although ziggurats were never as high as the tale suggests.

In ancient times, the most widely known of these structures was the Great Ziggurat at Ur. The city of Ur was the capital of the Sumerian culture and was, the Bible says, the home of Abraham.

Under the reign of King Ur-Nammu (c. 2060 B.C.), Ur became the most important city in Mesopotamia, populous and wealthy, an important trading center on the Euphrates River. In the middle of the city, Ur-Nammu built a high terraced ziggurat as the city's chief temple.

This imposing structure, towering above the low mud-brick houses of Ur, was built of sunbaked bricks set in a kind of mortar called bitumen and faced with glazed colored bricks. Ur-Nammu's original temple—built in honor of the moon goddess Nanna—rose in three receding tiers, with three wide frontal stairways leading to the top of the first tier.

Despite the angular appearance of the Ziggurat, there was not one straight line in the entire structure. The ancient Sumerians understood the technique of entasis, whereby supposedly straight lines were curved slightly so that a wall or pillar would appear straight when viewed from the ground.

It was the Babylonian king Nebuchadnezzar who made the Ziggurat at Ur the greatest ziggurat of the ancient world. After the Babylonians had captured the city, Nebuchadnezzar ordered that the Ziggurat be rebuilt. Where Ur-Nammu had built a pyramid of three tiers, Nebuchadnezzar built a seven-tiered tower. Each of the steps in the three frontal stairways was relaid bearing the name of this great king. A series of stairs and passages rising from the first tier gave the impression that a staircase wound around the tower in spiral fashion. Indeed, one could ascend to the apex via a spiral route, but a multitude of other paths were possible.

Nebuchadnezzar and a subsequent king, Nabonidus, more than doubled the height of Ur-Nammu's Ziggurat. At 160 feet, it became one of the highest structures in all Mesopotamia. The base itself—210 feet by 150 feet—was 40 feet high. At the top of the last tier, a couch and table were left for the moon goddess to use on her visits to earth.

The city of Ur was destroyed many times by conquerors and eventually abandoned. For thousands of years, the Great Ziggurat lay crumbling and covered with sand in the midst of a barren desert. During this century, however, the ruins of Ur were unearthed. The sandy rubble that the archaeologists found can hardly suggest the size and majesty of the ziggurat, the greatest structure of a great civilization.

A 35-pound peccary will take on a lynx—or even a locomotive

The peccary, an odd-looking piglike mammal whose habitat ranges from the southwestern United States to Brazil, looks like a curious cross among half a dozen animals. The peccary's head and body resemble a boar's; his flat nose looks like the end of an elephant's trunk. He has a scent gland like the skunk, runs on legs as delicate as a deer's, and has sharp, two-inch tusks in both his upper and lower jaws. But don't sidle up for a closer look—this queer fellow is one of the most dangerous fighters in the animal kingdom!

The peccary seldom measures more than forty inches in length and averages about thirty-five pounds, although in the tropics he may weigh as much as seventy pounds. Don't let this porcine char-

acter's size fool you, though. Those tusks can rip through flesh as if it were tissue paper. And where there's one peccary, there are usually a few dozen more. Against a combined peccary assault few animals have a fighting chance.

What makes the peccary even more dangerous is his unparalleled courage. This animal apparently never shows fear! Without batting an eye he will attack anything from a German shepherd to a jaguar. Peccaries have even been known to attack a railroad train!

A fungus looks like an egg-filled nest

Botanists in the seventeenth century were fascinated by a strange fungal growth that strongly resembles a small bird's nest with a clutch of tiny eggs. This fungus, *Cyathus striatus,* was thought by some to actually contain eggs. Others believed the egglike lumps inside the cup of the plant were seeds. Still others claimed to have seen these lumps give birth to live birds!

Of course, none of these claims were true. The spongy lumps within the acorn-sized cups are actually spore sacs, filled with thousands of tiny spores. The plant's resemblance to a bird's nest appears to be completely incidental. The fungus derives no benefit from its inadvertent mimicry.

The piranha is the world's most ferocious fish

In the streams and lakes of the South American tropics lurks a small, harmless-looking fish with a silver- and brown-speckled body—the piranha. But don't let the size of this creature fool you, for the piranha is the most ferocious fish to be found anywhere in the world. A school of these flesh-eaters can strip a man's skeleton clean in a matter of minutes!

The piranha's powerful jaws are lined with teeth as sharp as razor blades. Each tooth is shaped like a small triangle, and a row of them resembles the points of a king's crown. The natives of South America use these knifelike teeth as tips for their arrows.

Armed with these deadly razors, the piranha will not hesitate to attack any creature, no matter how large. One piranha would be troublesome enough, but these treacherous fish always attack their prey in schools of a hundred or more. And no animal of any size can withstand their vicious onslaught.

Strangely enough, piranhas will not bite the feet of cows crossing a stream in which they are swimming. But let a cow scrape its foot on a sharp rock and lose a drop of blood, and the piranhas will descend, ripping into the cow's feet until the poor animal keels over. And once the wounded cow has fallen, it will be only a matter of minutes before the blood-crazed piranhas have torn every bit of flesh from its bones!

The piranha's voracious appetite makes him an easy fish to catch, as he'll go for almost any bait. But if the other piranhas in a school see that one of their brothers has been hooked, they'll strip his bones clean too! A fisherman has to be quick indeed if he wants to find a piranha in one piece at the end of his line.

There is a crab that can kill a man

The giant spider crab—or *Macrocheira kampferi*—is undoubtedly the king of crustaceans. This nightmarish creature, who lives in the waters off the Ryukyu Islands southwest of Japan, stands three feet high and often weighs as much as thirty pounds. His powerful legs can spread as wide as twelve feet, and his savage claws have torn the flesh from men who have challenged him.

During the day, the spider crab lurks deep in his ocean home, but when the sun sets, he clambers ashore and ambles along the beach, looking like a grotesque creature from another planet. Japanese fishermen capture him with huge nets, and it often takes several men to hold the net once this monster has been snagged!

Yielding walked on stilts 22 feet high

He grew up in Great Yarmouth, England, among a family of circus performers, and he grew up dabbling in all sorts of circus stunts. After years of practice, Harry Yielding became expert on those awkward high-rise contraptions called stilts.

During the early 1900's, Yielding performed dressed as a clown, and how the crowd did roar when they saw him walking along on stilts 22 feet high—just about two stories above the ground.

Some snakes have two heads

Although many kinds of animals are known to have been born with two heads, such freaks are rare. But for some reason, an unusually large number of snakes are born with two complete heads growing out of one body. Many of these snakes also have two tails!

As a rule, both heads are fully developed. In such cases, two heads are definitely no better than one, for they certainly do not make the snake any smarter.

The king cobra can kill an elephant

The great king cobra of southeast Asia is one of the most dangerous creatures in the world. The largest of all poisonous snakes, an
adult king cobra may be as long as eighteen feet! Its poison sacs
are enormous, and the venom they secrete is one of the deadliest
known.

Moreover, the king cobra is one of the few snakes that will attack with little or no provocation. These serpents are especially
aggressive during mating and breeding time. During this period,
the male keeps close to the nest where the female is guarding her
eggs, and stands ready to attack anything appearing on the scene.
To be confronted by a king cobra with four or five feet of its length
reared upward would be a most nerve-shattering experience!

In Siam, even a huge elephant may fall victim to the attack of a
king cobra. The snake strikes either at the tender tip of the elephant's trunk, or at the thin-skinned spot where the elephant's toe-
nail joins its foot. An elephant thus bitten usually dies within three
hours!

58

Seeds of an arctic shrub bloomed after 10,000 years

For how long can a seed retain its generative capability? No one knows for sure, but it seems that under the right conditions a seed's potentiality for producing a new plant is almost eternal. For example, seeds of a sacred lotus plant, found in a peat deposit in Manchuria, were estimated by carbon dating to be about 1,400 years old. Nevertheless, when punctured and watered, the seeds rapidly germinated and produced plants!

If that seems incredible, consider this: in 1967, seeds of an arctic tundra shrub, *Lupinus arcticus,* were found in a frozen lemming burrow with animal remains established to be at least *10,000 years old!* When placed in conditions favorable to growth, the seeds germinated within 48 hours. There is no reason to believe that this remarkable generative power is the sole property of the arctic shrub.

Lillian Leitzel chinned the bar 27 times with one hand

By profession, Lillian Leitzel was an aerialist. She had performed in a number of circuses, including the famous Ringling Brothers and Barnum & Bailey production. This pint-sized acrobat—only 4 feet, 9 inches tall and weighing 95 pounds—was gifted with a strength that was almost unbelievable.

The record for one-handed chin-ups by a male athlete at the time was held by an Englishman named Cutler, who in 1878 completed 12 one-handed chin-ups. The difficulty of chinning with one hand is well recognized.

So when Lillian came to Hermann's Gym in Philadelphia in 1918 to work out with some acrobats, the gymnasts who were present scoffed at her claim that she could best the world's record for one-handed chin-ups. Lillian was 36 years old at the time.

Responding to the offer of a small, friendly wager to test her boast, Miss Leitzel took to the bar and clicked off 27 right-armed chin-ups in a row. After the pay-off and a short rest, Lillian had one more shock left for the bystanders. She leaped to the bar—this time with her LEFT hand!—and did 19 more one-handed chin-ups—a performance that again broke the male right-hand record.

The axolotl resembles a fish with legs

Few creatures, land or sea, are more improbably shaped than a Mexican amphibian known as the axolotl. This exotic lake dweller is unusual in that it permanently retains its larval features—as if it were a tadpole, which, instead of developing into a frog, simply grew into a larger tadpole. As a result, while other amphibians have lost their gills by the time they reach adulthood, most axolotls retain external gills throughout their lives. And a full-grown eight-inch axolotl looks much like a fish with stubby legs!

The toucan's bill is larger than its body

Toucans, a family of tropical American fruit-eating birds, have extremely large bills. Indeed, among some members of the family, the bill is actually bigger than the bird's body! This oversized beak gives the toucan an ungainly, somewhat comical appearance, but the thin-walled bill is light and not hard for the bird to carry.

The walking leaf is actually an insect

The Ceylonese insect known as the walking leaf can claim the world's most unusual camouflage. This odd creature so resembles a leaf that its presence in a tree cannot be detected. The insect's body is shaped and colored exactly like a leaf, and streaked with the vein-like markings of a leaf. The legs resemble smaller leaves,

62

and their slightly yellowed edges suggest that bits of leaf have been nibbled away by insects.

When the wind blows the tree in which the walking leaf makes its home, the insect wiggles gently, imitating perfectly the movements of wind-shaken leaves.

Theogenes fought and killed 1,425 opponents

In ancient days, the rulers of Greece and Rome would amuse themselves and their subjects through gladiatorial combats in which men fought to the death for the amusement of the spectators. History records that the greatest of these gladiators was a Greek called Theogenes, a native of Thasos.

Theogenes served a cruel prince named Thesus, who reigned about 900 B.C. Thesus delighted in sadistic spectacles and or-

dained a combat that was especially vicious. The two contestants—
if they can be called such—were placed facing each other, almost
nose to nose, each on a flat stone. Both men were strapped into
place. Their fists were encased in leather thongs which were studded with small, sharp metal spikes. At a given signal, they would
strike at each other, and the combat would continue, without rest,
until one of the contestants had been beaten to death.

During a long career, Theogenes—strong, skillful and savage—
faced 1,425 men and killed every one of them.

Bamboo is the world's largest grass plant

Can you imagine grass growing to the height of a 10-story building? Well, bamboo, whose woody, pole-like blades are sometimes used as crude fishing poles, belongs to the same plant family as the grass on your front lawn. And some species of bamboo grow in tufts to a height of 100 feet!

The growth rate of most bamboo plants is unbelievably rapid. The Molocca bamboo, for instance, can grow two feet in just 24 hours! But while the blades of the bamboo grow prodigiously, the growth of its flower is extremely slow—some bamboo plants do not flower until they are about 20 years old.

66

Of course, bamboo has many uses throughout the world in addition to fishing poles. The blades provide paper, fuel, and construction material for homes, furniture, utensils, plumbing pipes, and ship masts. And anyone who has ever dined in a Chinese restaurant is familiar with that Oriental delicacy, the pickled bamboo shoot.

The mongoose can kill the dreaded cobra

The deadly poisonous cobra strikes fear into the hearts of men and animals alike. And no wonder, for this snake's venom can kill a grown man within minutes. But there is one creature who'll never shrink from the cobra—the mongoose, an animal so plucky that he does not hesitate to attack this killer snake, four times larger than himself.

The mongoose, a native of India, is only about thirty inches long, with a sharp, pointed snout, short legs, tiny ears, and a tail as long as his body. A bright, friendly creature, the mongoose makes an excellent pet, and has been used throughout the world to combat rats. But it is in battle with the cobra that the mongoose earns his medal for bravery.

When a mongoose encounters a cobra, both become so tense that the air seems electrified. The huge cobra coils into a tense spring, and two flaps under its head puff out like a hood. Slowly the killer sways from side to side, its thin black tongue darting nervously in and out of its mouth.

In front of the cobra stands the mongoose, his short legs tense and his back arched like a spitting cat's. Every hair in his rough coat stands erect. Inching forward, he follows every movement of the cobra. One bite from those sharp fangs means instant death. Both animals seem to move together, their noses only a few inches apart.

Suddenly the snake strikes! The mongoose leaps backward at lightning speed, untouched. The cobra strikes again, and again the mongoose is quick enough to dodge him. The cobra lunges angrily, but time after time the clever little mongoose escapes his thrust, holding his ground and waiting for the cobra to tire.

When the snake begins to slow, the mongoose gets ready for his

own attack. He waits for the moment when the cobra does not withdraw its head quickly enough from one of its thrusts, then leaps forward and sinks his teeth into the back of the cobra's head.

Now the cobra's fangs are useless, for the mongoose has its head in an unshakable grip. The snake thrashes about madly, trying to coil its long body around the mongoose, but the furry creature keeps his jaws tightly clamped and hangs on. Not until the last breath has left the body of the cobra does the mongoose open his jaws for a well-earned rest. After the kill the mongoose will eat the entire snake, including the poison glands.

Some mongooses were considered sacred in ancient Egypt, and were often mummified. Before the introduction of domesticated cats, the mongoose was used to control rodents. One species, the Indian mongoose, was introduced into Jamaica and Martinique to combat viper infestation. The mongooses succeeded in controlling the snakes, but soon began preying on poultry. Eventually they became subject to vigorous control measures themselves.

Houdini stayed underwater in a sealed coffin an hour and a half

No locks, no chains, no manacles could hold Harry Houdini, the greatest escape artist of all time. Born as Erich Weiss in 1874, this boy from Appleton, Wisconsin, did not take long to make headlines.

His handcuff act became so famous that he was invited to "escape" from London's Scotland Yard. Superintendent Melville, chief of this, the most famous police force in the world, placed Houdini's arms around a pillar and then handcuffed him. Before Melville was out of the building, Houdini had freed himself and caught up to the chief!

Houdini could open any lock in the world in a few minutes. Once, on a tour through Europe, the continent's most famous locksmiths presented him with what they considered foolproof locks, the result of countless years of work. Houdini opened the locks so astonishingly fast that the master mechanics hardly knew what was happening.

During his European tour, Houdini escaped from jails in the cities of Liverpool, Amsterdam, Moscow, and The Hague. He duplicated these feats in almost every large city in the United States. The plain fact was that Houdini could enter or leave virtually any room, building, or cell at will.

His repertoire of escape acts fascinated millions all over the world. So uncanny were his performances that many believed Houdini possessed supernatural powers. Though Houdini vociferously denied being gifted with anything more than human attributes, his performances were so baffling that even his stout denials failed to squelch the talk. No one could fathom just how his stunts were accomplished; and it was not until after his death that his notebooks revealed how he contrived to do things which seemed beyond the powers of mortals.

One of his favorite stunts was to have himself bound by the police in a straitjacket used for the violently insane. No one, the police averred, could break out of this. But, in addition to the straitjacket, Harry had the police load him with iron shackles and ropes. Houdini was turned upside down, and hauled aloft in midair by means of a block and pulley. Then, in full sight of an astounded audience and an absolutely dumbfounded police detail, the incredible man would wriggle free.

How did he do it?

Houdini was one of the greatest athletes that ever lived. From

his early youth on, he had practiced body control. He could flex virtually every muscle in his body. His fingers had the strength of pliers; and his teeth were so strong that they could be used like a can opener. His strength was so great that he could bend iron bars, and his tactile sensibility so fantastic that while blindfolded he could tell the exact number of toothpicks he was kneeling on.

Still, how did Houdini get out of that straitjacket? Answer: He contracted his muscles in such a way that he could slip one hand out of its bonds. By similar contractions and maneuverings, he would set his limbs free. Then the great locksmith would free himself from his iron fetters.

Houdini left explicit directions as to just how the stunt could be accomplished, but so far no athlete has come along with enough physical dexterity to perform the feat.

Unsurpassed as a magician, Houdini displayed courage and daring equally unmatched. In the days when the airplane was still a new and unproved machine, Houdini jumped from one airplane to another—3,000 feet above the earth—*while handcuffed!*

On August 26, 1907, Houdini leaped off a bridge in San Francisco Bay with his hands tied behind his back and 75 pounds of ball and chain attached to his body. He came up out of the water unharmed.

On another occasion, Houdini was thrown into the East River in New York City, handcuffed inside a box to which 200 pounds of iron had been attached. But what were handcuffs, irons, and a river to Harry? He emerged within two minutes.

And then, on August 5, 1926, as if to cap all his former feats, he allowed himself to be sealed in a coffin which was then lowered into the waters of a swimming pool. Before a whole deputation of doctors and newsmen, he remained in the coffin under water *a full hour and a half!*

Immediately upon emerging, he was examined by physicians who all agreed that he had suffered no ill effects. Houdini contended that it was panic, not lack of air, which usually caused suffocation. His own muscle control was so phenomenal that he may have accomplished this stunt by means of suspended animation.

Yet despite the fact that the physicians gave Houdini a clean bill of health on August 5, 1926, the great magician and athlete did not live to see 1927.

There is a fish that climbs trees

The Australian walking fish has the best of two worlds. In the water it swims like any other fish. But this unusual fish's fins are bent in such a way that they can be used for walking, too. And the walking fish often does take a stroll, right out of the water, climbing the lower branches of trees at the water's edge and roosting there for hours! This peculiar fish seems capable of surviving quite well out of water, and even snacks on insects it finds in the trees.

The Alhambra is the fairy-tale fortress of Spain

An invitation to choose the most beautifully ornamented building in the world will naturally result in some difference of opinion, but a structure that is sure to top many lists is the exquisite citadel of the Alhambra, in Granada, Spain. This massive, sumptuously adorned complex of halls, towers, palaces, and courts is perhaps the finest example of the Moorish architecture that once dominated much of North Africa and Spain.

Resting atop a 35-acre plateau overlooking the historic city of

Granada, the Alhambra was for many years the home of the Moorish kings, serving as palace, fortress, and administrative headquarters for their Spanish empire. Built chiefly between 1230 and 1354, the Alhambra remained the last bulwark of Islam in Europe until Granada fell to the Spaniards in 1492.

During its tempestuous history the Alhambra has survived many calamities. The Spaniards destroyed much of the citadel when they recaptured Granada. In 1812, the towers of the fortress were blown up by Napoleon's troops, and in 1821, an earthquake heavily damaged the complex. Extensive restoration was undertaken after 1828, and today the 700-year-old Alhambra has regained much of its age-old charm.

The hilltop citadel is so extensive that it would take a visitor more than an hour to walk around the surrounding walls. (It is to these red-brick walls that the citadel owes its name, for "Alhambra" means "the Red" in Arabic.) But it is not size that earns the Alhambra its fame.

The older Moorish section of the complex—the Alcazaba—is a magnificent work of interior design and sculpture. Here, intricate carvings in marble, alabaster, plaster, and glazed tile adorn the walls and ceilings. Palm-like marble pillars and stalactite vaultings form shady arcades; rich mosaics decorate the halls; delicate fountains embellish the many sun-bathed courtyards.

The Palace of the Kings is perhaps the most elegant of the many buildings in the Alhambra. In the center of this palace is the famed Court of Lions, with its alabaster basin supported by white marble beasts. Nearby, in the Hall of Ambassadors—which boasts a 75-foot high dome—water spouts through the mouths of yawning lions. In the Court of Myrtles, a 10,000 square-foot pond glistens with the reflection of nearby myrtle trees, while underneath glimmering goldfish swim in the clear, still waters.

Through the years, the Alhambra has given birth to many legends, and ghosts are said to roam its quiet halls and courts. These spirits, according to legend, are the souls of the Alhambra's Moorish and Spanish residents, who would not forsake an earthly habitation of such heavenly beauty.

◈◈◈

The Astrodome was the first enclosed arena in which outdoor sports can be played

Upon its completion in 1965, the Harris County Sports Stadium in Houston, Texas—better known as the Astrodome—could lay claim to a number of impressive superlatives: the largest indoor arena in the world, roofed by the largest dome ever constructed, and the only sports stadium in the world that did not contain a single blade of grass.

The Astrodome is truly a landmark of modern engineering and a harbinger of things to come. The stadium sprawls over nine-

and-one-half acres and can seat 66,000 spectators. The surface of the field is covered with "Astroturf," a synthetic grass specially designed for the stadium. A scoreboard 474 feet long and four stories high features a 10,000-light screen that can show messages, shorts, cartoons, and anything else that can be put on film. But without doubt, the most revolutionary feature of the $20 million structure is the massive dome.

Constructed of transparent plastic panels supported by a steel lattice, the dome measures 710 feet in diameter and rises to the height of 208 feet over the playing field. The dome of the Pantheon in Rome—the largest dome of the ancient world—had only *4 percent* of the surface area of the Houston dome.

The dome also provides for year-round fair weather inside the stadium. An air-conditioning system circulates 6,600 tons of air *each minute,* and keeps the temperature inside the stadium at a constant 74 degrees. If on a humid day the air conditioning were turned off, an entrance of warmer air could cause it to rain in the stadium!

The mammoth dome has resulted in some unexpected problems for players in the stadium. During the first few baseball games played on the new field, players complained that balls hit

75

high into the air could not be seen against the backdrop of the dome. After a number of embarrassing muffs of fly balls by home-town players, the plastic panels of the dome were painted over to provide for better vision.

And, during a baseball game in the 1974 season, Philadelphia's Mike Schmidt did what had been considered impossible—he hit a ball against a public-address speaker affixed to the roof, 329 feet from the plate and 117 feet above the field. The would-be tape-measure however dropped in center field and Schmidt was held to a single.

In 1971, a domed stadium with a retractable panel overhead was completed in Irving, Texas, and the massive "Superdome" in New Orleans was ready a few years later. Undoubtedly, most of the sports stadiums built in the future will be domed—following the footsteps of the original, the Houston Astrodome.

⚜

Madame Regnier, though able to, did not talk for 30 years

Here is a cautionary tale for henpecked husbands. After reading about Madame Regnier, you may have second thoughts about telling your wife to button her lip.

Madame Regnier lived comfortably in Versailles as the wife of a French Royal Procurator, or crown attorney. One fine day in 1842, she was prattling about something or other when her husband admonished her, "Be silent, woman, you talk nonsense."

Madame Regnier stormed out of the room in a huff. For days afterward, she would not speak to her husband—nor to anyone else. At last, Monsieur Regnier went to his wife's chamber and abjectly apologized. His wife looked at him impassively, and said not a word.

Days stretched into weeks, and weeks into years, while Madame Regnier continued to hold her tongue. Even when her daughter came to ask for permission to marry, Madame Regnier only nodded her assent.

From that day in 1842 to her death 30 years later, Madame Regnier never uttered a sound.

Johnny Eck walked on his hands

Johnny Eck did not walk on his hands as a stunt; that was the only way he could get around, for he was born without a body below the waist. Johnny's arms were longer than his body, and so powerful that he could stand on one hand easily. He did have two feet, but they were malformed and useless.

Eck made his living in the circus, where he was bluntly called The Half Man. But Johnny lived a whole life; he was an excellent pianist and saxophonist who for a time had his own orchestra. He was also a first-rate actor, as he revealed in the films *Freaks* and *Tarzan*.

The cheetah is the fastest animal on earth

The swiftest man cannot run much faster than twenty-five miles an hour. The greyhound, fleetest of dogs, dashes at forty miles an hour. Racehorses can run from forty-five to fifty an hour, and the graceful antelope can leap along the ground at close to sixty. But no animal can keep pace with the most astonishing of all the world's runners—the magnificent jungle cat known as the cheetah.

78

Of all the great cats, the cheetah is the sleekest and most grace-ful. The golden coat of this Asian and African speed demon is cov-ered with black spots smaller than those of the leopard, and his legs are longer and thinner than the legs of the lion or tiger. When hunting an antelope, this fleet fellow can sprint at the phenomenal speed of *seventy miles an hour!* Once the cheetah decides to give chase, there is no animal that can escape him.

Stonehenge is an age-old enigma

One of the world's simplest, yet most astounding structures—Stonehenge—lies in eerie solitude on the marshy Salisbury Plain of Southwestern England. This remarkable construction of massive stones, built by an unknown people thousands of years ago, has been a puzzle to archaeologists and historians for centuries.

Although many of the stones have now fallen to earth, we know that the original arrangement of ditches, holes, and rock constructions was basically a series of concentric rings. A circular ditch 300 feet in diameter forms the outermost ring. Moving in toward the center, the next ring consists of 56 circular holes filled in with earth. These "Aubrey holes," so-called after the British antiquarian who studied Stonehenge—are each six feet wide and four feet deep. Within this ring are two circles comprised of smaller filled-in-holes, known as the Y and the Z holes.

The third ring is a circle of large Sarsen stones, each about 13½ feet high, arranged in post-and-lintel (upright-and-crossbeam) formations. The innermost ring is a circle of upright Bluestones, without lintels.

Within this Bluestone ring, we find a horseshoe of five hugh trilithons: massive stones as much as 24 feet high, with lintels across the top of the upright post stones. Each trilithon weighs over 30 tons! The horseshoe surrounds an ovoid formation of Bluestones, which is in turn wrapped around the center "altar" stone.

The amount of work required of a prehistoric people just to place the huge lintels atop the stone posts is staggering. But these hard rocks were not only hoisted; they were first smoothed with hammers. Incredibly, some of the rocks in Stonehenge came from quarries which were as far away as 30 miles! But the actual distance that the stones were carried was nearly twice that figure. Archaeologists have shown that the Bluestones must have been transported from the Prescelly Mountains in Wales, and that the simplest route must have covered at least 240 miles over land and water. Even with the use of rafts and rollers, this is a mind-boggling feat.

The heavier Sarsen stones were apparently brought from Marlborough Downs, about 20 miles distant from Stonehenge. This job would have required the work of 800 men.

The construction of the inner rings of Stonehenge is thought to have taken about seven years. The entire structure required an estimated total of 1.5 million man-hours of labor!

Why these prehistoric men worked so hard to construct this cu-

rious monolith remains a mystery. For centuries, it was thought that the structure was used as a pagan temple, for cremated bones were found in the Aubrey holes. But early in this century, the proposition was advanced that Stonehenge was constructed as a sort of seasonal clock, its main axis pointing directly toward the rising sun on midsummer day (June 24).

Each of the five post-and-lintel trilithons in the horseshoe frames the position of the sunset or sunrise on a key day. The Stonehenge structure could have been used by the ancient builders as a primitive alarm clock, advising when to plant and when to harvest. Calculations have shown that the risings and settings of the sun, as seen through the openings in the trilithons, are remarkably precise.

Tamerlane built pyramids from the skulls of his victims

In 1336, an obscure tribal chieftain, living near the Central Asian city of Samarkand, celebrated the birth of a son. The Mongol chieftain named his baby Timur. Later, when Timur was crippled by an arrow, he received his nickname, Timur-i-Leng, or Timur the Lame. To the Western world, he is more familiar as Tamerlane.

Making Samarkand his capital, Tamerlane set out on a decades-long campaign to subjugate the world to his rule. He creat-

ed an empire that stretched from the Ganges River in India to the very gates of Europe. Much of present-day Russia, including Moscow, was incorporated into his domains.

Merciless to his enemies, Tamerlane ravaged huge areas, reduced great cities to rubble, and slaughtered hundreds of thousands. Indeed, he left cruel testimonials to his victories by building great pyramids from the skulls of his victims—70,000 at Isfahan, 90,000 in Baghdad, and 100,000 at Delhi. At Sebsewar in Persia, the merciless monarch enclosed 2,000 live people inside a brick and mortar tomb.

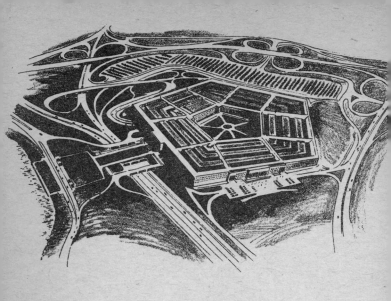

The Pentagon is the world's largest office building

Not long before America's entry into World War II, General B.B. Sommervell proposed the construction of a building to house all the agencies of the U.S. War Department. While many people viewed his proposal as an unnecessary extravagance for a nation that might soon become embroiled in a world war, others felt that this contingency was precisely the reason why the erection of centralized offices was imperative.

The latter view prevailed, and construction of the building began in September 1941, on a 34-acre site across the Potomac River from Washington, D.C. More than 13,000 workers were employed on the giant project; 6 million cubic yards of earth were moved; 41,492 pillars were sunk into the marshy earth; 410,000 cubic yards of concrete were poured; and 680,000 tons of sand and gravel were dredged from the bottom of the Potomac. War Department workers began moving into the building even before it was completed in January 1943.

Today, this building—known familiarly as the Pentagon—is synonymous with American military might, and stands as the largest office building in the world. Its total floor area could fill a square whose sides were *one-half mile*. The building consists of five con-

84

centric pentagons connected by ten "spokes." The outermost pentagon extends 921 feet on each of its five sides. The innermost pentagon encloses a large open courtyard. Paved courts and roads for delivery vehicles separate the other rings. The ingenious design of the building assures that, despite its size, no two offices are more than 1,800 feet—or six minutes walking time—apart from each other.

The Pentagon is truly a city in itself. Five stories plus a mezzanine and basement comprise a total area of 6½ million square feet, *three times* the floor area of the Empire State Building. Thirty miles of roads and interchanges girdle the site, while 17½ miles of corridors thread through the gigantic complex. Each day, the Pentagon houses more than 30,000 Defense Department workers.

Like any small city, the Pentagon has its Main Street. The long corridor known as the Concourse is lined with shops and showrooms of every kind, from shoeshine parlors and barber shops to airline agencies, a bus depot, and a post office. The two restaurants, six cafeterias, and ten snack bars alone employ a staff of 700.

The Pentagon's total cost of $83 million was considered astronomical at the time of its construction. Yet today, the rental of office space of an equal size would cost the government more than $20 million per day!

The electric ray shocks its prey

The queer-looking, circular-shaped fish called the electric ray has a most unusual method of catching its dinner. This soft-skinned creature is equipped with two muscular organs, one on each side of its head, which are capable of giving off strong electrical impulses. The ray captures its prey by "butting" the victim with these organs and thereby stunning or killing it with an electrical shock.

The ray also uses its electric organs to fight off enemies. Any creature that tangles with one of these deepwater fish is in for a rude shock, for the current produced by a large electric ray is powerful enough to kill a man!

Annie Taylor rode over Niagara Falls in a barrel

She was a childless, widowed, 43-year-old schoolteacher from Bay City, Michigan, and for the task at hand, her credentials were rather bland. For a first-time adventurer, her stakes were high.

On October 24, 1901, she would go over the 160-foot-high Horseshoe Falls in a barrel. Where others had failed, Annie Edson Taylor was willing to gamble. As it was, her life was going nowhere; if she succeeded, fame and fortune would follow.

On that big day, she made her entrance in a long black dress and fluttering hat. Only just before getting into her barrel would she change into a short skirt. For one thing she was prudish; for another, she weighed 160 pounds.

At Grass Island, Annie was lowered into the oak cask. From there, a rowboat took her out to where the currents would carry her to the Falls. Of course, it was no ordinary barrel. Bound by seven iron hoops, it was four and one-half feet high, four feet in diameter, and it weighted 160 pounds. A hundred pound anvil was tied to its bottom as an anchor, to keep the barrel upright when it floated.

The cheering throngs that gathered along the Niagara gave Annie the attention she craved. "Au revoir," she told them majestically, as she was turned loose. "I'll not say goodbye because I'm coming back."

As the barrel was picked up by the strong current, the throng fell silent and wondered.

The barrel bobbed and flipped, and then it splashed over the break. For Annie, strapped inside, there could be no strategy other than to use her strong muscles to brace herself. Luckily, when the barrel hit bottom, it bounced away from the Falls, and her aides fished her out. It wasn't until later that they learned she couldn't swim!

For Annie, there was immediate fame; but sadly, no fortune. Brokenhearted, she again became an unknown, but never again an adventurer.

෴

The Colossi of Memnon were statues that sang

In the 15th century B.C., the Egyptian king Amenhotep III erected a funeral temple near the city of Thebes, with two colossal stone statues guarding the entrance. In the following centuries, Egyptians were startled to hear, at each dawning, mysterious musical sounds emanating from one of the colossi!

The Greeks, equally baffled by the harp-like noises, named the 60-foot statues after the demigod Memnon. The daily song, they

believed, was the voice of Memnon greeting his mother Eos, the goddess of dawn.

After an earthquake damaged the two colossi, the Roman Emperor Septimius Severus had the statues repaired. But when the restoration was completed, the strange cries of Memnon ceased forever, as mysteriously as they had begun (although visitors today sometimes claim to hear eerie sounds emanating from the statues). Today the funeral temple is gone and the colossi stand on the desert alone—and silent.

The explanation for the strange cries? The rapid change in temperature as the desert sun rises at dawn produces strong air currents. These currents probably resounded through the loose joints of the colossus before Severus repaired it. The acoustic principles responsible for the curious sounds are similar to those of an organ pipe—making the statues the most oddly shaped organ pipes in history!

Philippe Petit walked a tightrope 110 stories high in the air

Early one morning in August, 1974, the skyline of lower Manhattan was altered in a small but stunning way: the twin towers of the World Trade Center, second tallest buildings in the world, were linked by a one-inch steel cable—and perched on that cable was a fellow named Philippe Petit. For 45 minutes, this 25-year-old French acrobat and juggler thrilled thousands of Manhattanites as he danced in mid-air at the dizzying height of 1,350 feet.

When Philippe grew bored with life at the top, he put his feet down on firmer terra and was promptly arrested for disorderly conduct. To police and newsmen, Petit made it clear that his conduct was, for him, the very model of order. In fact, his high-wire

antics 110 stories up were the culmination of 10 years' study and practice.

At the age of 15, Philippe quit school and joined the Omankowsky acrobatic troupe in the Loire Valley. In 1971, he became a celebrity in France by walking a high wire strung between the towers of Notre Dame cathedral. Shortly thereafter, he traveled to Sydney, Australia, and traversed a cable from one pylon of the giant Harbour Bridge to the other.

Petit's boldest venture required six months' study of the World Trade Center. He rented an apartment in New York and, with the help of friends, "cased the joint." Often, he and his friends had to don hard hats or pose as French architectural reporters to mask their real purpose. At last, in August 1974, they hid in one tower overnight and, with a crossbow, shot their cable across to the other tower. The next morning, Petit took his stratospheric stroll.

A reporter asked Petit the inevitable question: why did he do it? "I see three oranges," Petit responded, "I have to juggle. I see two towers, I have to walk."

~~~

Bees mistake the bee orchid flower for other bees

Most flowers produce nectar to lure insects to the reproductive parts of the plant, and thereby enlist the insect's aid in pollination. But some plants lack nectar. Nature has devised rather ingenious ways of attracting bees and other insects to these flowers. One of the most striking is that of the bee orchid, *Orchis apifera.*

The *Orchis* genus contains about 750 species of American and Caribbean orchid, most of which grow on or among other flowering plants. Since these other plants are most likely to be nectar producers, bees will be constantly flitting about in the vicinity of the orchid. How does the bee orchid lure bees from the nectar-secreting flowers to its own? Remarkable as it may seem, the bee orchid produces flowers that look just like bees!

Each bee orchid flower has three brightly colored petals, from the center of which protrudes a fuzzy, multi-colored growth that greatly resembles a particular large bee. This imitated insect is, in fact, an enemy of the pollinating bees found in the bee orchid's habitat. A male bee flying near the orchid mistakes the fuzzy growth for the enemy bee. It strikes at the plant in an effort to drive the invader from its territory. While striking at the flower the bee picks up and deposits pollen, thereby pollinating the orchid!

Woods disc-jockeyed for more than 11 days nonstop

Tommy Woods was an undergraduate at William Paterson College in Wayne, New Jersey, and also was active as a disc jockey on WPSC, his college's AM station. In December 1972, he came up with a wild idea: to go on the air and stay on longer than anyone ever had.

Woods began his broadcasting marathon at 8 a.m. on Monday, December 11, 1972, alternating hard-rock music with a steady flow of mellifluous DJ patter. Periodically, a registered nurse stopped in at the studio to check out Woods' physical condition. However, despite fatigue, eyestrain, and increasing hoarseness, Woods remained awake and on the job for more than 11 consecutive days.

Before very long, Tommy became a hero on campus and in the surrounding community. An audience of millions who lived outside WPSC's small listening area vividly followed his progress as reported by TV newsmen in nearby New York City.

Finally, at 4 p.m. on December 22, 1972, Tommy Woods played his last record, said a few final, elated words, and signed off. He had been on the air continuously for a total of 272 hours—a world's record.

Calverley's 55-foot basketball shot tied a major tournament game

In basketball, it's size that counts. That's why oddsmakers made the five giants from Bowling Green a 12-point favorite over little Rhode Island State on March 14, 1946, in the opening game of the National Invitation Tournament in New York City. A record 18,548 fans crowded the old 49th Street Madison Square Garden. Standing five-foot-ten, Ernie Calverley of underdog Rhode Island jumped against the six-foot-eleven Don Otten of the Ohioans at the tipoff.

Rhode Island State surprised, and the game was close all the way. On 13 occasions, the score was tied. Then, with 3:20 minutes left on the clock, the Ohioans lost Otten on fouls. But Bowling Green still had the height to control the game. With only ten sec-

onds remaining, Bowling Green held onto a 74-72 lead. As the tension mounted, Rhode Island moved the ball down the court. In order to stop the advance, a Bowling Green player barged in and risked a one-shot foul—a pretty smart maneuver, for under the rules in effect at the time, if Rhode Island chose to shoot the foul, they would lose the game even if their player had sunk his foul shot. Time would just run out.

So Rhode Island elected to waive the foul shot, and took possession of the ball. Only three seconds were left now to move the ball the full length of the court, and make a basket. It was a practical impossibility. The Bowling Green players tightened their web around the Rhode Islanders. Somehow, Calverley broke loose. He was well behind the mid-court line when a teammate threw the ball to him. Almost without pause, Calverley let fly for the basket —a target which seemed miles away. Here was a desperation shot if there ever was one. But Ernie's long-distance two-hander executed a perfect parabola and descended cleanly through the mesh, not even touching the rim. Calverley had tied the game, and the Garden broke loose in pandemonium!

After that, in the overtime, Bowling Green, still in the throes of shock, was no match for the little Rams, who won by a final score of 82 to 79.

Opinions differ as to the exact point from which Calverley let fly. The ball zoomed at least 50 feet—no one disputes that. However, some observers estimated the distance at 65 feet. A Garden official close to the scene claimed that he recalled the exact point from which the ball took off, and the officials measured it at 55 feet. But wherever it was, Ernie had certainly made the most famous basketball shot in history.

Mildred Didrikson Zaharias was a champion in track, golf, and baseball

In 1950, the Associated Press polled its sports writers and sportscasters to choose the greatest female athlete of the first half of the 20th century. The Associated Press people selected "Babe" Didrikson Zaharias (née Mildred Didrikson). It was an easy choice, for the Babe from Beaumont, Texas, was generally considered to be the greatest woman athlete who ever lived.

The Babe first came into national prominence as a basketball player. During her teens, she was nominated on All-America teams for three straight years, though she stood merely a shade over five feet tall. In one of her games, she scored over 100 points.

In 1932, Mildred entered the Amateur Athletic Union national track championships as a one-woman track team representing the Employers Casualty Company of Dallas. Other competing teams consisted of 10 to 22 members. Yet on that weekend in Chicago, the 18-year-old Babe entered eight events and scored points in seven. She won five outright, setting three world records in the process. Before the close of 1932, the 105-pound girl added two Olympic titles to her collection of medals, winning the javelin throw and the hurdles.

In baseball, Mildred toured the country with a professional barnstorming team—a team composed only of men; and she played only against men. But the Babe could throw a ball almost 300 feet on a straight line.

As the Babe grew older, she found her favorite sport in golf. During her career, she won more than 50 major tournaments. She once ran up a streak of 17 tournament victories. With the help of a wind, she once drove a ball 346 yards!

In 1954, after undergoing an operation for cancer, Mildred Zaharias won her third National Open. Had her brilliant career not been cut short by the dread killer, Mrs. Zaharias, who passed away in 1956 at the age of 43, would have undoubtedly added still more laurels.

The squid throws up a smokescreen

The cuttlefish, or squid, has a singular way of escaping from its enemies. When closely pressed, the squid shoots out a cloud of black sepia. Leaving its enemy in the dark, the clever cuttlefish then makes its getaway.

The Shayad Tower symbolizes modern Iran

In 1971, Iran—which describes itself as the world's oldest monarchy—celebrated the 2,500th anniversary of the first Persian Empire. Heads of state from around the world came to view the gala celebration staged near Persepolis by Shah Mohammed Reza

Pahlavi, the reigning monarch since 1941. And in Teheran, the capital city, construction began on a striking new monumental tower, the Shayad, to commemorate the anniversary.

The Shayad Tower was completed in 1972, and stands today as the gateway to bustling Teheran. The bold design of the tower combines both modern and traditional forms, symbolizing the illustrious past and the promising future of this oil-rich nation.

Morris skipped rope 22,806 times in two hours

Thomas Morris had a strange mode of locomotion. He got a great kick out of skipping rope, and once he traveled from Melbourne to Adelaide and back, a distance of 1,000 miles, skipping rope all the way.

On November 21, 1937, Morris began skipping before a timer in Sydney, Australia. Morris wanted to make some sort of an official test as to his prowess and speed. He set off at a rate of 200 beats a minute, better than three skips every single second. The pace was so grueling that his audience was stunned into silence. After one hour had passed, it was recorded that Morris had completed 12,000 skips. Since he was still fresh, he decided to go on for another hour, and without missing a beat, he continued. At the finish, his timers were as worn out as he was. For they had tallied an astonishing 22,806 skips. If each skip were accounted as the step of an average man, Thomas Morris, in those two hours, would have walked about 12 miles!

Spitz won seven Olympic gold medals in swimming

When Mark Spitz arrived in Munich, West Germany for the 1972 Olympic Games, the whole world was watching him. The dark, handsome, powerfully built Spitz had already established himself as the most outstanding swimmer of modern times. He had been swimming since early childhood, and set his first U.S. record in 1960—which still stands—in a 50-yard butterfly competition for nine- and ten-year olds.

Spitz, who lives in Carmichael, California, had won two gold medals at the 1968 Olympic Games in Mexico City, and at various times had broken 28 world freestyle and butterfly records. In 1971 alone, he had won four national and two collegiate championships in the United States, and had set seven world and two U.S. records.

For the 1972 Olympics, Spitz was entered in four individual competitions and three relay events. He had a chance to win seven gold medals, two more than anyone had ever won at a single session of the Olympic Games.

All the spectators at Munich's 9,000-seat Schwimhalle were aware of this record-shattering possibility as Spitz leapt into the pool for his first test, the 200-meter butterfly, on the afternoon of August 28, 1972. Spitz reached the finish line first, beating the world record which he himself had set several weeks before at the U.S. Olympic Trials in Chicago.

A few hours later, as a member of the winning U.S. team in the 400-meter freestyle relay, Spitz won his second gold medal. The next evening, finishing first in the 200-meter freestyle, he won his third.

Spitz won two more medals on September 1: the 100-meter butterfly, in which he set a new world record, and the 800-meter freestyle relay, in which he anchored the winning U.S. team. On September 3, by winning the 100-meter freestyle, Spitz became the first Olympic athlete ever to garner so many gold medals at one Olympiad.

Finally, on September 4, swimming the butterfly leg for the U.S. team in the 400-meter medley relay, the 22-year-old Spitz won his seventh medal.

Knievel, on a motorcycle, jumped over 20 automobiles

From the mountains of Butte, Montana, came Robert Craig Knievel, daredevil stunt rider, who, to dramatize his billing, chose the nickname of "Evel." And Knievel certainly had an eye for the dramatic.

On May 30, 1967, at the Ascot Speedway in Gardena, California, Evel Knievel gunned his Triumph motorcycle and jumped off a ramp at a speed of 80 miles an hour. That allowed him to clear 16 automobiles standing in a row.

To prove the stunt was no fluke, Knievel attempted 16 cars again—four more times, to be exact. Twice he made it. The other two times proved how dangerous the feat is: once he broke his lower spine, the other time he suffered a brain concussion.

This type of daredeviltry earned the 29-year-old Montanan about $100,000 in 1967. Now Knievel planned a bigger spectacular. The ornamental fountains at *Caesar's Palace,* one of the largest hostelries and casinos of Las Vegas, had been advertised as the largest privately owned fountains in the world. On New Year's Day, 1968, Knievel set forth to scale these waterspouts.

A ramp was especially built for him. He took off at 100 miles an hour and catapulted his 198-pound body to a height of 30 feet. He was definitely over the fountains with a leap of 150 feet. But evil pursued Knievel, and as his Triumph motorcycle hit the descending ramp at a speed of 70 miles an hour, the front wheel went askew, and Knievel lost control. He sped along over the neighboring asphalt parking lot for 165 feet, and then wound up in the hospital.

Was Evel daunted? Not so that anybody could make out. Four years later, he cleared 20 cars!

All European and North American eels are born—and die—in the same place

There are hundreds of species of eel to be found in the streams and rivers of Europe and North America, but all of these snakelike fish have one remarkable thing in common: They were all spawned in the same part of the ocean!

The Sargasso Sea is a large, relatively calm area of the North Atlantic noted for the dense seaweed that covers its waters. Once a year millions of eels leave their freshwater homes and swim to the Sargasso Sea, where they lay their eggs—and die. Ocean currents carry the newborn, tadpole-like eels to the continental shelves off Europe and North America to mature. The following spring, millions of eels form a dense mass, miles long, in many rivers and streams as they swim inland.

Some of these elongated fish will live as long as fifteen years in fresh water before returning to the Sargasso Sea to spawn and die. Thus, aside from those eels that are killed by man or other creatures while living in their streams, eels are not only born in the same place, but die there as well!

Oddly enough, drought will not prevent these fish from migrating back to the Sargasso Sea. Although classified as a fish, the eel can breathe through its skin when out of water, and therefore can migrate great distances over land!

Grass of Parnassus fools flies with fake nectar

All that glistens is not gold, and in the plant world all glistening, sweet-smelling liquid is not nectar—as flies soon discover during their visits to a grass of Parnassus plant. This floral faker, known also as Parnassia, has "decoy" nectaries which dupe flies into fertilizing its flower.

In most plants of the Parnassia genus, approximately five sterile stamens alternate with an equal number of fertile stamens. The sterile decoys each bear a button-like gland which secretes a fluid resembling nectar. Flies are attracted to the glistening, scented droplets of this liquid only to discover they've been fooled in their search for nectar.

But there is a reward for the insect visitors after all. Real nectar collects in depressions on the upper surface of the petals, near the center of the flower. Once attracted to the plant by the glistening buttons, the flies continue into the flower for their reward. On their way they brush against the sex organs, and fertilize the plant.

The kangaroo rat never drinks water

The kangaroo rat, a tiny desert rodent, is in no way related to its much larger namesake, the kangaroo. In fact, in nature the two creatures have never laid eyes on each other—the three-inch kangaroo rat makes his home in the arid southwestern United States, while his seven-foot marsupial mammal can be found only in Australia. The only connection between the two is the kangaroo rat's extraordinary leaping abilities.

This remarkable rodent has proportionately the same long, powerful legs as the kangaroo, and the same strong tail that the animal can use to sit on. Catapulting up from the ground like a popping watch spring, the kangaroo rat can jump right over a man's outstretched hand, with phenomenal accuracy, and land directly on top of a grasshopper. And a battle between two kangaroo rats is one of the strangest spectacles imaginable, for the two combatants fight by leaping into the air like mice on pogo sticks and

striking at each other with their sharp claws while in midair!

But the most peculiar thing of all about this little leaper is that he never, in his entire life, takes a drink of water—or any other liquid, for that matter. Living in the dry, hot deserts of the Southwest, where water is scarce, the frisky little fellow gets moisture from prairie roots and herbs. These plants, no juicier than the vegetables you eat at dinner, provide all the liquid the kangaroo rat needs.

Knox bowled a perfect game without seeing the pins

Bowling a perfect game, though admittedly rare, is not an unheard-of feat. Most every top professional has bowled a perfect game at one time or other during his career. But nobody has ever equaled the feat of Bill Knox, who in 1933 knocked down the ten-pins 12 times in a row without ever seeing them.

Knox had a special screen built at the Olney Alleys of Philadelphia and instructed two pin boys to hold the screen about one foot above the foul line. The screen would hide the pins from the sight of the bowler and would even block off the sight of the lane itself. But the fans sitting in the stands could see over the top of the screen. Knox's purpose was to show bowlers the effectiveness of "spot" bowling—choosing a point on which to lay down the ball.

His control was so unbelievable that the sphere was in the perfect groove 12 times out of 12. Bill Knox had bowled a perfect game without ever seeing his target.

The mystery of the stone faces on Easter Island is still unsolved

On Easter Day, 1722, the Dutch explorer Jakob Roggeven chanced upon a small, remote island in the South Pacific, almost 2,500 miles from the coast of South America. There he found—amid the craters of extinct volcanoes and a small tribe of stone-age people—a collection of mysterious faces gazing stoically towards the ocean. Even today archaeologists have not solved all the puzzles posed by the immense monoliths of Easter Island.

The massive heads are set against the gentle slopes of the island's volcanic ridges. Imbedded deep in the soil, the almost identical heads rise from 10 to 40 feet above the ground, and many are estimated to weigh close to 50 tons! In all, over 600 statues dot the island, forming a strange gallery of somber faces on many of the island's slopes.

The figures were carved of tufa, a soft volcanic stone that was quarried in the center of one of the island's volcanoes—Rano Raraku. When explorers discovered the deserted quarry, they found close to 150 additional statues that had never been moved to their intended places on the hillside. These figures, in various stages of completion, and the tools that still lay scattered about the quarry, gave evidence that the work on the monoliths had been interrupted quite suddenly and had never been resumed.

The more archaeologists investigated the island, the more they were startled by their discoveries. Bones and ash were found bur-

ied in the earth at the foot of the statues. Flat red rocks that lay beside many of the monoliths were shown to be "hats" or "topknots" that at one time rested on top of the heads. And when archaeologists began digging deeper in the soil around the faces, they discovered that the unknown sculptors had carved not merely faces but also full-bodied figures, many of which were now imbedded 30 feet in the ground!

How were the massive stones carried distances of up to 10 miles from the Rano Raraku quarry without losing their smoothly polished finish? How were the gigantic "topknots" hoisted atop the heads without pulleys? How did the bodies come to be so deeply imbedded in the earth? How long ago were the statues carved, and by whom, and for what reason? Why was the work halted so abruptly? All these are questions that decades of research and debate have not answered definitively.

Fanny Blankers-Koen won four Olympic gold medals

When Fanny Blankers-Koen stepped up to the starting line at Wembley Stadium in London during the 1948 Olympics, few in the stands would guess that this attractive blonde was a housewife and the mother of two young children. When the gun blasted off,

the trim Hollander dashed to the forefront, and stayed there until
she reached the tape—the winner in the 100-meter dash in 11.9
seconds.

Mrs. Blankers-Koen then proceeded to carry off the honors in
the 200-meter dash, covering the distance in 24.4 seconds.

In negotiating the 80-meter hurdles, she established an Olympic
record of 11.2 seconds.

And to top off her performance, Fanny led the 400-meter relay
team from the Netherlands to a first-place victory. The Dutch
housewife had carted off four gold medals within a week's time—
an Olympic record.

But there is more to be said. Unfortunately, the Olympic rules limited the blonde streak to entering three individual events. At a time when Fanny Blankers-Koen held the world's record in both the broad jump and the high jump, had she been allowed to compete in these events, it is safe to say that she would have done fairly well.

∽∾⚘∾∽

The Strasbourg Cathedral contains the most elaborate clock ever built

Visitors to Strasbourg, France will marvel at the gothic splendor of the city's main cathedral, whose 466-foot tower is the tallest medieval tower still standing in Europe. But the modern visitor is likely to be most intrigued by a more recent addition to the age-old cathedral: an astronomic clock that may well be the most elaborate timepiece ever constructed.

The Strasbourg Cathedral, completed in 1439, has displayed an astronomic clock since 1352. But the ingenious device that now stands in the cathedral is the work of Jean-Baptiste Schwilgué, who completed his clock in 1842. This intricate structural masterpiece is run by hundreds of hidden gears, and the various dials and figurines on the outside of the clock form a small mechanical circus, with performances every fifteen minutes.

Near the top of the timepiece, the four ages of man are represented by figures of an infant, adolescent, warrior, and old man. Every quarter hour, each figure in turn takes two steps forward, rings a bell, and then disappears. About the quartet, figures of the 12 apostles appear through a small doorway. A mechanical cock greets the arrival of the apostles by raising its head, bristling its plumage, opening its beak, and crowing three times. Two angels swing their hammers against bells, adding to the confusion of chimes and moving figures.

Below the angels, seven figures—representing the seven days of the week and the seven inner planets—revolve in a ring, with one figure visible each day. The clock also boasts an angel with a working hourglass, a figure of Christ, a revolving celestial globe, a figure of death who rings a bell with a bone, and sculptured panels

depicting Copernicus, Uranus (the goddes of astronomy), the
Resurrection, the Creation, and Schwilgué himself.

The clock faces illustrate three distinct methods of time-keep-
ing: standard time, in hours and minutes; apparent time, indicat-
ed by the sunrise and sunset, the phases of the moon, the coming

of eclipses, and other movements of the sun and moon; and sidereal time, governed by the movement of the stars through the signs of the zodiac. Together, the various time-telling devices comprise not only one of the most intricate and amusing clocks in the world, but also one of the most accurate.

◈

The leaves of the compass plant point north and south

If you're ever lost in the country, a compass plant could come in handy. This North American herb, also known as rosinweed, orients its leaves to the points of the compass. The leaf surfaces almost always point towards the rising or setting sun—that is, east or west—with the surfaces exactly parellel to the sun's rays at midday. Thus, the ends of the leaves usually point due north or south as dependably as the needle of a compass!

◈

King Otto of Bavaria shot a peasant a day

Here's the life of another King Otto (see page 176), this time a real one from Bavaria. Otto gained the crown in 1886, but he was hardly fit to rule his subjects. For the previous 14 years, his raving lunacy had forced his family to keep him in a locked room. This constraint did not seem to bother Otto too much, because it did allow him the privacy necessary for his conferences with the spirits who lived in his dresser drawers.

One of Otto's more peculiar notions was that if he shot a peasant a day, he could keep the doctor away. The Mad King was enabled to gratify this whim by the compliance of two loyal guards. One guard would daily load Otto's gun with blanks, while the other would don peasant garb and hide in the bushes outside the King's window. When Otto would appear at the window with pistol poised, the "peasant" would emerge from his hiding place and amiably drop dead at the sound of the shot.

At Chichen Itza, thousands of victims were hurled to their death

In the centuries preceding Columbus's voyage to the New World, the Maya Indians developed a highly advanced civilization centering in the Yucatan Peninsula of Mexico. One of their greatest cities was Chichen Itza, "the city of the Itzas at the mouth of the wells." First settled by the Mayas in 514, this city was once the home of close to 100,000 people, and the mecca of Mayan pilgrims throughout Central America.

Chichen Itza was abandoned in the 15th century and subsequently overgrown with jungle. But from these ruins modern man has been able to learn much about not only Mayan architecture, but the customs of these ancient people as well.

While all wooden and earthen structures in Chichen Itza had disintegrated long before this century, the stone buildings remain almost intact. These massive white-stone constructions are ornamented with heavy decorative sculpture—with the feathered serpent as the most prominent motif—and enclose dark, cramped interiors.

Among the most striking structures of the ancient city is the Caracol, a round stone tower 41 feet high which probably served as an astronomical observatory, for the Mayas were skilled astronomers. A large stadium and game courts are located near the center of the city. Nearby is the Temple of a Thousand Columns, which gets its name from the rows of stone columns that surround the building.

Yet the most interesting by far of all Chichen Itza's monumental structures is the sacrificial complex leading to the deep well from which the city gets its name. The Mayas built their city beside two such wells: one was used to draw water for irrigation and drinking; the second—called the Cenote—was considered sacred, the home of the rain god Yum-Chac. Into the depth of this sacred well the Mayas hurled precious artifacts and, often, human sacrifices.

111

Near the Temple of a Thousand Columns, a tall step pyramid rises 100 feet in nine tiers, topped with a small stone shrine. In this shrine began the procession that took the young sacrificial victims to the well of the rain god. Ninety steps lead down one side of the pyramid to a quarter-mile stone causeway.

The solemn procession followed this causeway to a small altar at the edge of the 60-foot well. There, the victims were plunged down into a 60-foot ravine to appease the bloodthirsty Yum-Chac. At the bottom of the ravine lay the well, whose murky waters were sixty feet deep and over 150 feet wide.

The walls of the ravine are too steep to have allowed the victims, had they survived the plummet into the well, to escape the clutches of the rain god. However, these victims were usually so laden with jade and metal that it is unlikely any of them survived the 60-foot plunge or the waters below. When the sacred well was dredged earlier in this century, many precious objects were discovered among the bones in the thick silt below the waters.

Georges Clemenceau slept fully dressed

Georges Clemenceau (1841-1929) was known as "The Tiger" for his passionate concern with the welfare of France. He was twice his nation's premier, the second time rallying the dispirited French to victory in World War I.

Clemenceau had the peculiar habit of going to bed each night in a full dress suit: trousers, waistcoat, coat, and even gloves! The only concessions to comfort he allowed were the exchange of his starched shirt for an unstarched one, and the wearing of slippers instead of street shoes.

Clemenceau slept in this manner his whole life; but in his final days, he was thwarted in his intention of meeting his Maker fully prepared. In a half-conscious state, he could offer no resistance to the doctors who removed his formal clothes.

LeBel jumped over 17 barrels on skates

The rules of jumping on skates are quite specific: the barrels must measure 16 inches in diameter and be 30 inches wide; the skater must clear the barrels cleanly without touching any one of them. Since the hazard of crashing is great, the barrels are made of a fibrous composition that has some give to it. Nevertheless, failing to jump over a barrel at great speed involves danger to limb and neck. Only those of great courage and confidence essay this sport.

On December 18, 1965, Kenneth LeBel, a native of Lake Placid, New York, and Jacques Favero, a Canadian, met at the Grossinger Hotel in Liberty, New York, to compete in a match which would determine the world's champion barrel jumper. After Favero had catapulted himself over 16 barrels, the 180-pound LeBel circled the rink a couple of times to get up speed. Then he roared down the 200-foot straightway, leaped, and sailed through the air at a speed of 40 miles an hour. LeBel had jumped over 17 barrels, darting through the air for a distance of 28 feet and 8 inches!

Cardinal Mezzofanti learned 114 languages

Joseph Caspar of Bologna, Italy, had very little schooling. At an early age, he was apprenticed to a carpenter. While working in the shop one day in the mid-1780's, he heard a priest next door giving lessons in Greek and Latin to some students. Though he was not even in the class, and had never seen a book in either language, the young carpenter proved to be the best pupil. In a short while, he was able to speak both languages fluently.

The would-be carpenter later became priest and eventually earned the title of Cardinal Mezzofanti. He spent most of his life studying languages, learning to speak at least 53 languages with considerable fluency. He spoke 61 additional tongues not quite so well, and understood 72 more dialects, although he could not speak them.

The only language to provide Cardinal Mezzofanti any difficulty at all was Chinese, which took the master linguist all of four months to learn!

How much does one have to travel to learn languages? Cardinal Mezzofanti never once left Italy in his whole life!

A pigeon can find its home from fifteen hundred miles away

The homing instinct of the carrier pigeon is so strongly developed that these birds can fly more than a thousand miles over unfamiliar territory and never fail to find their way home.

A pigeon's training begins at the age of three months. Released by its keeper a short distance from home, the young bird quickly flies back to its dovecote. The distance is gradually increased until the pigeon is able to return from more than 1,500 miles away to the spot where it was bred.

Messages placed in a metal container can be attached to the foot of the bird. Unless the homing pigeon, a small target indeed, is shot as it wings its way through the air, there is little chance of intercepting the message it carries.

The Temple at Madura is ornamented with 30 million idols

According to legend, the Hindu temple of Siva at Madura, India, is adorned with *30 million* intricately molded idols. This figure may indeed be an exaggeration, but even if there are "only" 1 million idols, Madura would still be one of the most elaborately ornamented temples in the world.

In the 16th and 17th centuries, the city of Madura was the capital of a large Hindu kingdom. In this city, King Tirumula began the construction of a massive walled temple complex. But Tirumula's temple was not to be one of delicate grace and beauty to honor a glorious and benign Hindu deity. Instead, the temple at Madura was a shrine to Siva, the Destroyer, and depicted the god in all his grotesque forms.

The walls of this nightmarish temple are over 1,000 feet long on each side and surround a maze of courts, halls, and colonnades. Ten pyramid-like gate towers rise to the height of a 20-story building, and each is completely covered with tier upon tier of densely jumbled idols. These images—molded of plaster, painted in garish hues of red and green, and coated with rancid butter—depict gods and goddesses and demons and monsters of all shapes and forms.

Simply to count all the idols on the towers and walls at Madura would take years. The task of molding and painting them must surely have required decades of work by countless sculptors.

Hall scored three goals in three and one half minutes of soccer

Soccer is a low-scoring game—especially in international matches. Generally, a score will run two goals or three goals a game, rarely as many as six. So the nonpareil outburst by a British stalwart, G.W. Hall, must rank among the greatest soccer feats of all time.

On November 16, 1938, England stunned its arch-rival Ireland in a one-sided contest that ended 7-0. What was remarkable was that three of those goals were scored by one player in the space of three and a half minutes. Never in major competition has any soccer player tallied in such a rat-a-tat fashion.

118

With England leading 1-0 in the first half, 40,000 witnesses at the Old Trafford stadium in Manchester saw London's inside-right turn the trick. Hall scored his initial tally set up in front of the goal-mouth by his brilliant team-mate, Stanley Matthews. Moments after the ensuing kickoff, Hall scored again—this time on a low corner shot from inside left. When the ball was put back in play, the Irish goalie was determined to stop the barrage. Charged with more enthusiasm than wisdom, he ventured out too far after Hall, and the net was an easy target. Hall tallied again, and the crowd went wild!

But Hall wasn't through. Ten minutes after the intermission, the Britisher connected again with a fine spinning shot that he hooked in with his back turned to the goalie.

And Willie scored still once more when the redoubtable Matthews, dribbling past two men, flicked a pass which Hall converted. That made five for Willie for the afternoon.

Priscilla Lauther was known as the Monkey Girl

On a rainy, windswept night in 1929, Carl Lauther was about to close up his tent show for lack of customers. Just as he went to turn out the lights, a drenched, shabbily dressed couple walked up to him. The woman carried a bundle in her arms. She threw back the folds of the blanket to reveal an incredible sight—a baby girl covered from head to foot with silky black hair.

The couple knew that their child was "different," and thought that since Lauther was a circus showman, he might be interested in taking her. Lauther immediately recognized the gold mine that this infant represented, and gladly took the girl from her relieved parents. Lauther and his wife named the child Priscilla, and legally adopted her.

Priscilla grew to be a healthy, well-developed teenager and the star attraction of the Lauthers' show. She played with her pet chimpanzees before the crowds, and was billed as "The Monkey Girl Who Lives with Apes." Apart from the hair which covered her body, Priscilla's only physical problem was that she had two sets of teeth, one row behind the other.

In 1946, when Priscilla was 17, a wealthy woman offered to pay for all of Priscilla's dental needs. In exchange, the woman asked only one thing: she wanted to crossbreed one of her pet apes with Priscilla!

At this point, an unusual "knight in shining armor" arrived on the scene—a young circus performer whose skin affliction caused him to be labeled "The Alligator Boy." He and Priscilla married, and performed together as "The World's Strangest Couple," which they surely were.

This incredible marriage brought crowds streaming to the carnival. With the new-found profits, Priscilla's parents could easily afford the dental operations she required. These were successful, and The Monkey Woman and The Aligator Boy lived, as far as anybody knows, happily thereafter.

The tern migrates halfway around the globe

The Arctic tern leads a strange life indeed, spending three months of each year in the Arctic regions, three months in the Antarctic—and almost six months in the air! For this small gull-like bird flies one of the longest migratory journeys made by any creature.

The tern summers in the Arctic, then heads south in the fall. Traveling at a leisurely thirty to thirty-five miles an hour, stopping to rest and eat on the ocean and on land, the tern meanders southward for three months. After a trip that may total eleven thousand miles, the well-traveled fellow at last reaches the neighborhood of the South Pole.

But when spring arrives, the tern is off again on another eleven thousand-mile journey back to his Arctic home. This remarkable bird thus flies a round trip covering as much as 22,000 miles—and he repeats his feat each year!

120

The stonefish has poisonous fins

The stonefish gets its name from the hideous wartlike texture of its skin, which looks as if it were studded with small pebbles. In fact, the stonefish can easily be mistaken for a pile of stones, for it spends most of its time almost motionless on the bottom of the tropical ocean, or lounging amid the coral and rocks. But pity the creature that disturbs this ugly sluggard! The stonefish's dorsal fin contains a venom gland, and through a groove in this fin the stonefish can shoot a deadly poison—sometimes powerful enough to kill a man!

The Gateway Arch is the world's tallest monument

In the early 1960's, a massive construction project was undertaken in St. Louis, Missouri, to reconstruct much of the city's downtown area—particularly the Mississippi riverfront. The new structures in the restored area included a 51,000-seat sports stadium and the imposing Gateway Arch. Upon its completion in 1965, the Arch became the tallest monument in the world.

The Arch was built to commemorate the westward expansion of the United States after the Louisiana Purchase of 1803, and especially the important role St. Louis played in that expansion as the gateway to the West. The towering, graceful structure—designed by the noted architect Eero Saarinen—spans 630 feet along the Mississippi riverfront. The height of the arch is also 630 feet, which makes the monument as tall as a *60-story building!*

The vivid sight of the sun's rays glistening on the shining steel is visible from miles away. And each year thousands of visitors ride in 40-passenger cars that take them to the top of the colossal arch for a breathtaking view of surrounding Missouri and Illinois.

Though initially the arch met with some opposition from the citizenry at large, it has now come to be regarded as one of the finest achievements in modern architecture.

The mouse deer can stand in the palm of a hand

If you were to come upon a mouse deer in the Malayan jungle, you might think you'd stumbled into the land of the Lilliputians. For this creature is the image of the full-sized deer that roams the forests of America, identical in almost every detail with its much larger counterpart—except that the fully grown mouse deer stands less than one foot high!

This miniature deer is incredibly dainty and beautiful. His legs are so slender they seem like sticks of fragile glass. His delicate head is even smaller than the head of a rat, and if the two animals meet, the rat would look the huskier of the pair.

For his size, the mouse deer is one of the fastest creatures in the jungle. He runs with a peculiar motion, something like the bouncing of a rubber ball, ending each few steps in a sprightly little leap.

**Finn ran 100 yards in a sack in 14.4
seconds**

Nowadays, sack races are usually held as entertainments during
church outings or family picnics. But there was a time earlier in
this century when the sack race was a regular event on many track
and field schedules. The winner of such a contest scored just as
many points for his team as did a pole vaulter or a miler.

The best sack racer ever was an Irish-American from Brooklyn,
New York, by the name of Johnny Finn. On May 1, 1929, in New
York's 106th Regiment Armory, Finn competed in the 100-yard
race—the popular distance in sack events. Each of the contestants
lined up at the starting line, each one standing up to his neck in a
cumbersome burlap bag. The oddness of grown-up men en-
meshed in a such a get-up brought the usual laughter from the

crowd. However, with the crack of the starter's gun, everyone settled down to business. The athletes waddled, hopped, stumbled, and shuffled down the straightway.

At the finish, it was Finn as usual who was home first, breaking the tape at 14.4 seconds for a world's record. Just how fast that was may be gathered from the fact that on that same night—in the same meet—the 100-yard dash was won by a sprinter who covered the distance in 10.4 seconds.

Chichester sailed around the world alone

During the 1920's and 1930's, a spare, simple-looking English real-estate magnate turned to flying. Combining skill with daring, Francis Chichester established a number of aerial records. However, one of his attempts led to his being invalided for five years. As soon as he was able to get around again, Chichester attempted a solo flight around the world, crashed into some telephone poles in Japan, and broke 13 bones, Finally, he decided to look elsewhere for his thrills.

When he was 52, Chichester set forth on the greatest adventure of his life: to sail around the world alone in his boat, the Gipsy Moth IV, a sea-going ketch 53 feet in length—a boat that was normally manned by a crew of six.

On August 27, 1966, Francis Chichester departed from Plymouth, England. It was to be a harrowing trip. When he reached the treacherous waters of Cape Horn, squalls as strong as 100 knots an hour rocked his ketch and frigid waves spilled over the deck. Five times the cockpit was flooded, and Chichester was constantly in mortal peril.

Yet against all odds, the man succeeded. Francis covered 28,500 miles in a voyage that took him 226 days. Queen Elizabeth was so impressed with his exploit that she knighted him while he was still at sea.

Chichester's trip must certainly stand as one of the greatest physical performances ever made by a man in his fifties.

The peanut's fruits mature underground

When we think of a bizarre plant, we're likely to call to mind some exotic giant from the tropical rain forests. But often the plants that surround us have intriguing properties, too. The peanut is a good example. It is one of the few plants with the property of geocarpy, the underground ripening of fruit.

After pollination, the peanut stalks holding the fertilized ovaries elongate and bend downward. Eventually this growth pushes the seed pods into the soil, where they mature. But the length to which these stalks can grow is limited, and the peanut plant has a mysterious way of "knowing" before pollination if the seed pods will be able to reach the ground. Thus, if the plant has grown too high, the upper parts of the plant will simply not produce any seeds!

Another "talent" exhibited by the peanut is versatility; George Washington Carver discovered several hundred uses for the various parts of the peanut plant.

Daisy Ashford wrote a best-selling novel as a child

In 1909, Daisy Ashford won renown throughout the English-speaking world with her novel *The Young Visiters*. An uproariously funny book, *The Young Visiters* scored an immediate success and topped the 200,000 mark in sales.

Miss Ashford's characters were favorably compared with those of Charles Dickens. Her deft portrait of late Victorian society provides incisive social comment on the foibles of the period. But what really makes Miss Ashford so incredible is that she wrote this novel when she was only nine years old. Despite this early literary triumph, Daisy Ashford never wrote another book!

Fitzsimmons KO'd a man 140 pounds heavier than himself

On April 30, 1900, in Brooklyn, New York, Robert Fitzsimmons, a 37-year-old Englishman, fought Edward Dunkhorst, an American heavyweight. "Ruby Robert," as he was known, stood five feet 11¾ inches in height, and didn't look particularly robust at 165 pounds. Dunkhorst tipped the scales at a hearty 305.

Fitzsimmons' strategy was clear. He would move in with a flurry of punches and then back off from his opponent, move in again and then back off. He intended to wear Dunkhorst down.

127

In the second round, Ruby Robert dropped the big, hulking Dunkhorst to the floor, and Ed never got up to continue the battle. Fitzsimmons had beaten a man who outweighed him by 140 pounds!

During his career, Ruby Robert, one of the great fistic names of all time, held the championship in the middle-weight class, the light-heavyweight class, and the heavyweight class.

The genius of Sidis, a child prodigy, fizzled out as he grew older

William J. Sidis, Jr., son of an American psychiatrist, became his father's star pupil a short time after his birth in 1898. At the age of six months, William knew the alphabet. By the time he was two, the boy could read and write. By his eighth year, young Bill had completed 11 years of grammar school and high school. At nine, the boy entered Harvard University.

As an 11-year-old student at Harvard, Sidis delivered a lecture displaying his knowledge of the highly complicated fourth dimension, thoroughly amazing the members of the mathematics department. At the age of 16, he was graduated with honors, and at 19 he was made a full professor of mathematics.

Yet despite his virtually unprecedented scholastic achievements, Sidis failed to live up to the promise of his early years. At 26, the student who had been so brilliant in higher mathematics was discovered operating an adding machine in a New York store. In 1943, a lonely ex-genius, he died in a New York rooming house.

The "Scottish Brothers" had one body and two heads

In the late 15th century, the court of James III of Scotland featured one of the oddities of the age—the "Scottish Brothers." When young King James learned of a set of twins joined at the abdomen, with two legs, four arms, and two heads, he had the children sent to the royal court. James wanted not only to satisfy his curiosity, but also to save the freaks from possible harm in the rural backwater from which they came.

King James arranged for the "Scottish Brothers" to be educated, including special training in art, music, and foreign languages. As the brothers matured, they each developed passionate and sometimes contrary tastes in music, art, and letters. These antagonisms often reached the point of physical mayhem. The sight of the brothers' four fists raining blows upon their two heads must have looked like a helicopter.

The brothers lived under royal protection for the rest of their lives, until they were 28. One brother died five days before the other, who moaned piteously as he crept about the castle gardens, half dead and half alive.

Swahn competed in the Olympic games at age 73

As an accountant employed in the Stockholm office of the Swedish Telegram Bureau, Oscar G. Swahn must have seemed an ordinary enough person, but he was one of the finest riflemen who ever lived. During his 65-year career, he won more than 500 awards and prizes and he was a member of the Swedish shooting team at four meetings of the Olympic Games. His specialty was the running-deer event.

At the Paris Games in 1900, Swahn won a gold medal in the single-shot running-deer event. In 1908, at the London Games—where at age 61 he was the oldest participant in any event—Swahn again won a gold medal in the single-shot running-deer, a bronze medal in the double-shot, and helped win a gold medal for Sweden in the team single-shot event.

The 1912 Games were held in Stockholm, Swahn's home town. Competing before the admiring eyes of thousands of his countrymen, Swahn, again the oldest competitor, was a member of the gold-medal team in the single-shot running-deer event, and the bronze-medal team in the double-shot.

Because of World War I, the Olympic Games were not held in 1916. But at the first peacetime session of the Games, held in Antwerp in 1920, Swahn competed at the amazing age of 73. He helped win a team bronze medal for Sweden in the single-shot, and a team silver medal in the double-shot.

Four years later, Swahn once more qualified for the Swedish shooting team. At the last minute, though, he was prevented by illness from participating in the Games. He died in 1927 at the age of 80.

Brown beat six professional fighters on the same night

Most boxers prefer their fights just one at a time, with weeks of rest and training periods in between.

But consider the case of Preston Brown of Philadelphia's

Broadway Athletic Club. One night in 1913, he announced that he would take on all comers, and no fewer than six ring-wise professionals arose from the ranks.

Every one of the challengers was bigger than Brown. Nonetheless the plucky 125-pounder took them on—one by one—and he walloped them all. He knocked out five of the six—in early rounds, no less. The sixth challanger lost on a decision.

⟨∾⟩

A foot-long sea hedgehog can kill a 20-foot shark

The sea hedgehog owes its name to the unusual composition of its skin. Like its landlubber cousin's, the sea hedgehog's fur is studded with sharp quills. Thanks to these quills, this sea creature, which measures less than a foot in length, is capable of killing a relatively huge enemy, the shark!

The sea hedgehog is often attacked and swallowed by sharks. Once it is in the belly of the shark, though, the sea hedgehog inflates its prickly body as if it were a balloon. The spearlike points penetrate the stomach of the shark and rip a hole through the monster's body. The sea hedgehog then calmly swims through the gap, leaving a fatally-wounded shark behind.

⟨∾⟩

Ernst walked from Constantinople to Calcutta and back in 59 days

Mensen Ernst grew up in the heart of Norway's fjord country. Though he earned his living as a sailor, he made his fame as a landlubber. He traversed Europe, Asia, and Africa on foot in unbelievable record time.

Little jaunts like a march from Paris to Moscow, or a hike from

Germany to Greece, were nothing for this Norwegian. He took those kinds of walks in stride, so to speak.

In 1836, when he was 37 years old, the sturdy Viking took off from Constantinople (now Istanbul) and headed for Calcutta in eastern India. The two cities were 2,800 miles apart. The trip meant crossing mountains, rivers, badlands, and the deserts of the Middle East. Ernst trekked along for almost 100 miles each day; and when he reached Calcutta he hardly took time off for a nap, but did an about-face to return to Constantinople. He completed his two-way trip in 59 days, an over-all average of four miles an hour day and night, counting sleeping hours, too.

This was a 5,589-mile hike accomplished at a time when many roads were not paved, and through areas where in some localities there were no roads at all. No man has ever equaled this walking achievement.

The chimpanzee can be taught sign language

Chimpanzees are undoubtedly the most intelligent non-human creatures in the world. It has long been known that any normally bright chimp can be taught to use simple tools such as the brush, cup, spoon, and hammer, and to mimic many human gestures. But recent experiments have shown that this remarkable ape has a learning potential far greater than had been previously supposed. Some chimps have even been taught to use forms of language!

In one experiment, a young chimp was taught a sign language with which he communicated with his trainer. This chimp was able not only to learn the correct signs for forty different subjects, but to grasp and use language concepts such as the adjective, verb, and adverb as well!

Another experiment showed that a chimpanzee can construct "sentences" once he learns a number of words. A chimp taught the correlation between certain words and a set of marked tokens was

able to place these tokens in such an order as to make a statement expressing what the chimp felt, even though these "sentences" were usually as simple as: "me want banana now please."

And still another experiment demonstrated that these smartest of all nonhumans could be taught to use money. Chimps learned that by placing a certain chip in a slot machine they could obtain grapes from the machine. It didn't take these clever creatures long before they began working for their chips, hoarding them—even fighting over them!

St. Peter's is the largest Christian church in the world

For sheer size, the church of St. Peter's in Rome is an extraordinary structure, easily outstripping such great cathedrals as Rheims, Chartres, and Notre Dame de Paris. Yet St. Peter's is also one of the world's most renowned works of architecture, and boasts painting and sculpture by the greatest artists of the Renaissance. The crowning glory of an age, St. Peter's remains today the center of the Roman Catholic Church.

Even the site upon which St. Peter's rests is historically significant. It was here, on the left bank of the Tiber, that the Roman Emperor Nero built a large amphitheater to house his gory spectacles, in which thousands of Christians died for the viewing pleasure of the Roman masses. Among these victims was St. Peter, the Church's first pope, who was crucified and buried in a mass grave outside the amphitheater.

In the 4th century, the Roman Emperor Constantine the Great —the first Christian emperor—built a small church in place of the old amphitheater. The altar of this church was placed directly over the supposed site of Peter's grave. Here many popes and emperors—among them Charlemagne—were crowned.

By the 15th century, Constantine's church was crumbling, and portions were rebuilt by Pope Nicholas V. Then, in 1506, at the height of the Renaissance, Pope Julian II decided to construct a new church on the site, a grand church worthy of the most powerful institution in the world.

Julian's plan called for a church large enough to hold 80,000 people—at that time, the entire population of Rome! A monumental design by the architect Bramante was accepted, and the greatest construction project in the Church's history was underway.

Bramante's church was so large and elaborate that 12 architects spent most of their lives working on the project. Raphael was in charge of construction for a time. Michelangelo supervised the building of the immense dome, but he—like most of the artists who worked on the project—never lived to see the church completed.

It wasn't until 1626, 120 years after construction began, that St. Peter's was dedicated. And it was another 40 years before the vast piazza and colonnades in front of the church were finished. In memory of the thousands of Christians who had died in Nero's

arena, an Egyptian obelisk that had stood in the center of the amphitheater was placed in the center of this piazza.

The main section of St. Peter's is 700 feet long and 450 feet wide, enclosing an area of over seven acres. Most of the world's cathedrals could fit inside without difficulty. Imagine a church this large topped by a roof as high as a 15-story building!

Within the church are 44 altars, the largest being a huge work of bronze upon which only the Pope himself may conduct mass. Three-hundred-ninety statues—most of them quite large—adorn the interior and exterior. But the most extraordinary feature of the church is the massive dome designed by Michelangelo. For hundreds of years, the dome of St. Peter's stood as the world's largest.

It is high enough to enclose the Capitol Building in Washington, D.C.—with 65 feet to spare!

Today, St. Peter's is only a part of the Vatican complex, with its numerous chapels, palaces, and gardens. But St. Peter's remains the greatest structure of the Vatican and the greatest church in the world.

A camel can go without water for almost a week

The dromedary, or one-humped camel, is so well designed for desert travel that he has been called the "Ship of the Desert." While other animals would probably collapse from heat and thirst after a few hours in the desert sun, a fully laden dromedary can walk well over two hundred miles in the most parched desert—without so much as one drink of water!

It is the unusual arrangement of the camel's stomachs that suits him so well for desert travel. The dromedary's stomachs—he has several, like the cow—are lined with millions of tiny storage cells, which can retain enough water to sustain the hardy beast for close to a week.

The camel can also go without food for long periods of time. The hump on a dromedary's back holds layers of fat, and serves as a sort of food storehouse. Thus, a well-fed camel has a larger hump than an overworked, poorly fed one.

This walking reservoir has another talent that makes him particularly useful in the desert—a marvelous sense of smell. Camels can sniff out water holes from miles away. Many caravans would have perished if their "Ships of the Desert" hadn't found water for them.

Plaisted won a professional rowing race at age 74

When he was 17, Frederick Plaisted won his first professional rowing race, and with it $500 in cash. But it was his very last stake race—a race that occurred 57 years later—that earned Plaisted immortality.

Fred was 74 years old when he and two old professional rivals, Jim Ten Eyck and Jim Riley, set up a match in Saratoga to determine who was the best of the three. Plaisted, then of Philadelphia, found a backer who put up $1,000 for him. (Plaisted was finicky about his backers, and for good reason. He once went to China to race for $10,000 cash, only to find after his victory that $10,000 cash in Chinese money was worth $10 in American specie.)

At 5 a.m. on that morning in 1924, the three lined up before a crowd of 1,000 onlookers. The course was marked off at three miles—a good-sized race for rowers of any age bracket. The betting was fairly heavy.

For the first half-mile all three rowers seemed surprisingly strong. Then Ten Eyck, the rowing coach at Syracuse, faded.

Riley, who had the advantage of being on his own course, pressed on, staying within striking distance of Plaisted.

But Plaisted, once a 240-pounder who now weighed in at 185, had power to burn. By the halfway mark, Fred was away by himself. As Riley grew weaker at the finish, Plaisted came in with considerable margin to spare, in the impressive time of 21 minutes, 4 seconds.

Fred Plaisted never raced again for money, but he did race again. He celebrated his 89th birthday by defeating John B. Kelly, an ex-Olympic champion and a much younger man, in a race on the Schuylkill in Philadelphia.

On his 91st birthday, Fred admitted to rowing three miles every other day, just to keep in shape. When interviewed, he said, "Technically, I am a better rower now than I ever was." He died when he was 95.

The squirting cucumber can propel its seeds up to 40 feet

The squirting lapel flower is an old practical joke, but there are many specimens of the plant kingdom that do indeed squirt liquid—some with great force. Among these is the squirting cucumber, a Mediterranean plant that depends upon the propulsion of fruit juice for the dispersal of its seeds.

The seeds of the squirting cucumber are contained in an oval fruit about one and a half inches long. When the fruit is ripe the inner tissue forms a liquid, in which the seeds float. The "cucumber" swells with liquid to the bursting point, then explodes and propels the juice and seed mixture through a small hole punched in the end of the fruit. The explosion is powerful enough to propel the seeds as far as 40 feet from the plant!

The armadillo rolls itself into an armor-plated ball

Various species of a bizzare-looking mammal known as the armadillo abound in the Western Hemisphere from the southwest United States to Argentina, and range in size from the fifteen-inch, twelve-ounce "pink fairy" armadillo to the five-foot, one 125-pound "giant." All species have one thing in common: a body encased in a hard shell of small bony plates. When threatened by another creature, an armadillo will often roll itself up into a tightly compressed ball, pulling in its head and limbs and leaving little to attack but a mass of armor plates. One species, known as the three-banded armadillo, can curl up in a perfect ball, *completely* protected by its bony shell!

The armadillo is a nocturnal animal, and spends most of the day inside its burrow, a complex of underground passageways that it builds by scratching through the earth with its sharp, heavy claws. An armadillo's burrow complex can be twenty feet long, with as many as twelve entrances. At night this miniature tank leaves its underground home and searches out its dinner of insects, frogs, plants, and small reptiles. Gifted with a keen sense of smell, an armadillo can detect an insect grub up to five inches below the ground!

One ferret can rid a farm of rats

You probably know that the expression *ferret out* means *search out* or *dig out*. But did you realize that the words originally had a more limited meaning: to use a ferret to flush another animal from hiding? For until the use of modern rodent poisons became widespread, farmers depended on the ferret—a white, cat-sized relative of the weasel—to rid their fields of destructive pests. And this furry creature is so well suited to the task you'd think nature placed him on earth to do nothing but help the harried farmer!

The ferret has a slender, silky body just perfect for crawling down into narrow ratholes, and a pair of pink eyes that can see in almost total darkness. Ferrets are trained and kept in cages on the

farm, and when a field begins to get a bit overcrowded with vermin, the walking rat trap is brought to the rescue.

The farmer stuffs a ferret into his pocket and goes in seach of ratholes. When he finds one, he places the ferret before it and gives the little fellow a shove. Like a tiger stalking its prey in the underbrush, the ferret crawls through the dark underground passages until he finds the rat, and then snarls savagely.

The animals swipe at each other with their claws, but the rat soon learns that he is no match for his ferocious adversary. The rodent flees towards daylight, but the relentless ferret is right on his tail. No sooner does the terror-stricken rat emerge from the hole than his attacker leaps and sinks his teeth into the rodent's throat.

By systematically attending to all the holes and rock crevices in his field with these white wonders, a farmer can, well, ferret out all his rat enemies—and all he had to do himself is sit on the ground and wait!

There is a fungus that can capture an animal

A carnivorous fungus known as *Zoophagus insidians* engages in a sort of microscopic fishing expedition to catch its dinner. Along the main stem of the fungus are short branches, called hyphae, which are appetizing to minute aquatic animals known as rotifers. When a rotifer bites into a hyphae, the tip of the branch begins to swell inside the animal. Like a fish snared on a hook, the rotifer is helplessly trapped on the swollen end of the branch!

As the victim struggles to escape, the fungus shoots out a glob of mucilage that helps to hold the prey. The fungus later ingests nutrients from the dead animal.

Crickets chirp more quickly in warm weather

The male cricket produces his characteristic chirping noises by rubbing his forewings together. The higher the air temperature, the greater the number of chirps he generates per minute. Thus, you can tell the temperature by counting a cricket's chirps! Provided that the thermometer reads between forty-five and eighty degrees, count the number of chirps you hear in fifteen seconds. Then add thirty-seven to this number. The result will tell you the exact air temperature at the time!

The flying squirrel does not have wings

The name "flying squirrel" is a misnomer, for no mammal except the bat is capable of true flight. In fact, the flying squirrel does not even have wings. But these popeyed rodents could aptly be called "gliding squirrels," for that's just what they do—glide like paper airplanes from tree to tree.

Stretched between the squirrel's front and hind legs are thin, parachutelike flaps of skin, one on each side. By spreading these flaps wide as he pushes off from a branch, the flying squirrel can coast gracefully on air currents to another tree. Although some of these creatures are over two feet long, they can often soar between branches more than one hundred feet apart!

Al Herpin never slept in his 94 years of life

Most of us get a full eight hours' sleep each night to perform at peak the following day. Others get along quite nicely with as little as three to four hours' shuteye. But it is universally agreed that a human being must eventually sleep, just as he must eat and drink. In fact, doctors are fond of saying that sleep is the brain's food; starve the brain and you die.

So what are we to make of the strange case of Al Herpin? A 90-year-old handyman of average intelligence and excellent health, Herpin lived in a tarpaper shanty outside Trenton, New Jersey, in the 1940's. When word spread of this ancient who claimed he had never slept, legions of doctors marched to his door, determined to expose the fraud and thus buttress their own medical theories.

Inside Al Herpin's house, the doctors found a rocking chair and a table—but no bed, no hammock, no cot, nothing on which a man might lie down. For weeks on end, medics attended Herpin in relays, waiting for the man to sneak a few winks. He never did. Naturally, after a hard day's work at odd jobs, he would be tired. But his way of resting was to sit in his rocker and read seven newspapers thoroughly until he felt refreshed.

Herpin himself contended that the cause of his lifelong insomnia was an injury his mother had suffered just a few days before delivering the infant Al.

Herpin finally closed his eyes for eternal sleep on January 3, 1947, at the age of 94.

The Lithops plant is a "living stone"

Camouflage is uncommon in the plant kingdom. The bizarre shapes and color arrangements displayed by many species serve mainly to attract pollinators, rarely to protect the plant from potential harm. However, there is one remarkable family of plants that has developed a highly effective form of camouflage. These plants resemble rocks and pebbles so closely that they are commonly called "living stones."

These stone mimics are found in the barren, rock-strewn wastes of southern Africa, where the paucity of vegetative life would make an undisguised plant an easy prey for the birds, baboons, and other creatures that feed in the area. The "living stones," however, blend in perfectly with this rocky landscape. One species resembles pieces of greenish granite; another mimics limestone; another, quartz. Perhaps the most remarkable members of the family are those of the Lithops group, which closely resemble small pebbles.

Lithops plants are stemless, and their leaves are buried in the soil so that only the tips are visible. These tips form a fleshy, roundish structure, which is flat on top and almost flush against the ground. Their mottled shades of gray, brown, and red mimic the coloration of the pebbles that surround them. Frequently, the plants spread sideways, so that one plant may appear to be several stones.

The Lithops are distinguished by a narrow slit which runs across the flat upper surface of the leaf. During the flowering season, tall flower stems rise from the slit. But when the dry season returns, the flowers disappear, and the mimics once again become indistinguishable from the stony landscape.

One termite queen can produce half a billion children

Termites, like ants and bees, live together in large colonies. Some species of this wood-eating insect build their homes belowground, while others construct massive nests aboveground, using wood, leaves, and a sticky substance from their mouths. Such steeple-shaped nests can rise as high as twenty feet! But there is one thing that all termite colonies have in common—there is only one queen.

Termite queens are easily the longest-lived insect specimens in the world—some survive for more than fifty years. And a healthy queen can produce over thirty thousand eggs in one day. That means that over the course of her lifetime, a queen termite could conceivably give birth to about a *half a billion* children!

The frogfish catches its prey with rod and reel

Fishermen have nothing on the frogfish, for this peculiar sea creature catches its supper with a built-in hook and line. Long strands that resemble thin fishing lines are rooted to the top of the frogfish's head. Lying in ambush, the frogfish casts out the strands, and smaller fish, taking these dangling threads to be swimming worms, go for a nibble. Once caught on the barbed end of the strand, the would-be worm eaters are immediately gobbled up by the frogfish.

**Beatty entered an arena that contained 50
lions and tigers**

The greatest animal trainer who ever lived was just 5 feet, 5 inches
tall. Until his death in 1965, Clyde Beatty was considered to be
without peer in the handling of wild beasts. He would enter a cage
armed only with a .38-caliber pistol that could hardly kill a flea.
His weapon was loaded only with blanks which he used at times
simply to scare his charges.

During a long career, the curly-headed Midwesterner faced
thousands and thousands of lions, tigers, leopards, bears, ocelots
and jaguars. Of course, this exposure yielded its untoward results.
Time and again, Beatty was clawed and he bore the scars from
over 100 maulings by wild cats, some of which weighed over 500
pounds.

Beatty's routine called for him to spend about a quarter of an

hour locked up in a cage with anywhere from 12 to 24 lions and tigers. But on one occasion, he undertook to handle 50 of the big cats. Nobody, either before or since, has ever essayed such a feat. But Beatty was really a master.

Holding a whip in one hand and a chair in the other, he kept all the animals in their places. Using the crack of his whip, low whispers, blank shots from his pistol, and even screams, he kept this full menagerie of roaring, snarling beasts under control.

The feat is all the more remarkable when it is realized that it is virtually impossible for a man to keep 50 caged lions and tigers within the range of his peripheral vision. Clyde solved this problem by keeping his chair tilted toward the direction where he wasn't looking, while the animals in the range of his glare felt the constant threat of being whipped. Whenever a lion threatened to lunge at Beatty, he froze stark still, stared the animal down, and held up his chair for protection. With his other hand, he threatened with his whip.

However, before the day was over, even the unusually game Clyde Beatty admitted that 50 animals on a rampage at one time would have been even too much for him to manage.

He never tried it again.

Mistletoe is known as the "vampire plant"

The custom of kissing underneath a sprig of mistletoe has earned the plant a charming reputation. But there is another—hardly charming—side to this evergreen which is suggested by its gruesome nickname: "vampire plant." For as a vampire was thought to suck blood from its victims, so the parasitic mistletoe sucks the life's blood from its host plant.

Herbs and shrubs of the mistletoe family—there are 35 species in all—send modified roots, called haustoria, into the tissue of the host plant to obtain nourishment. Although mistletoe prefers trees, it can live on many different plants. Occasionally a mistletoe will even attach itself to another mistletoe! But the parasite can sap the strength from its host, and thus bring about the death of both plants.

Birds often assist in carrying mistletoe seeds to suitable host plants. As birds feed on the plant's waxy white berries, the seeds contained inside stick to their bills and feet. The birds scrape off the seeds on the bark of trees, and when the seeds germinate, the roots bore into the tissue of the newfound host.

One dwarf species of mistletoe has another way of spreading its progeny: its berries explode when ripe, sending seeds as far as 50 feet from the parent plant!

A wealth of folklore and superstition has surrounded mistletoe. Though often fatal to fellow plants, mistletoe was thought of as a panacea for many human ills. The plant was sacred to several early sects, among them the Druids, who apparently originated the custom of kissing underneath a sprig of the "vampire plant."

Mosienko scored three goals in 21 seconds in a professional hockey game

In a lackluster professional hockey game in New York on March 23, 1952, the New York Rangers were pitted against the Chicago Black Hawks. The visitors were behind, 6 to 2, in the final period; some of the more than 3,000 fans who had come to see the game had already left the dreary spectacle. The Rangers had the game virtually won. What was there to stay for?

Then, with less than 14 minutes to play, right wing Bill Mosienko, thirty years old, picked up a pass from teammate Gus Bodnar and rapped in a goal.

On the ensuing face-off, Bodnar again got the puck to Mosienko, and the pint-sized 160-pounder smashed in goal No. 2. Only 11 seconds had separated the two tallies. The score now stood at 6 to 4.

On the next face-off, Mosienko skated into position. There was Bodnar again with another perfect pass. The Chicago player faked a defenseman out of position and blasted a long shot at the befuddled goalie, who stood helpless as the puck passed by him into the net for Mosienko's third score! This trio of tallies took all of 21 seconds—a record that is likely to hold for many a year.

Mosienko was done for the night, but his teammates were not. Infused with new life, they scored still another two goals against their now fog-eyed opponents to win an amazing 7 to 6 victory.

The scarlet pimpernel can predict the weather

The next time you go camping in the woods and would like the weather forecast in the morning, don't turn on a transistor radio—try to find a scarlet pimpernel. The scarlet, white, or purplish flowers of this herb will close up in the morning if rain or cloudy weather is in store, and expand if the weather will be fair. This prophetic property has earned the scarlet pimpernel the nickname of "poor man's weatherglass."

The Winchester Mansion is the most bizarre house ever built

Mrs. Sara Winchester's mansion near San José, California, is without doubt the most bizarre residence ever constructed. This house—which began as a modest-sized dwelling in 1884—grew year by year into a nonsensical maze of rooms, corridors, and stairways, many of which served no function whatsoever. The most imaginative amusement-park funhouse could hardly compete with Mrs. Winchester's mansion in its freakishness of design.

This mansion owes its outlandish construction to Mrs. Winchester's odd fear—she was convinced she would die if she stopped adding rooms to her house! The wealthy woman was so certain of her conviction that she kept scores of carpenters, masons, and

plumbers busy every day for nearly 38 years.

Some rooms in the mansion were built and furnished with the elegance of a royal palace, with gold and silver chandeliers, stained-glass windows, inlaid floors, and satin-covered walls. Other parts of the house were constructed only so that the eccentric resident could hear the reassuring bang of hammers. Some rooms measured only a few inches wide, and some stairways led nowhere. The mad mansion contained 2,000 doors and 10,000 windows, many of which opened onto blank walls! The eight-story house also boasted three elevators, 48 fireplaces, nine kitchens, and miles of secret passages and hallways.

When Mrs. Winchester died in 1922 at the age of 85, her mansion contained 160 rooms and sprawled over six acres. The total cost of this insane structure was over $5,000,000!

The aardvark "plants" and fertilizes the desert melon's seeds

The desert melon has a curious relationship with an animal that shares its South African habitat, the aardvark. The melon provides water for the aardvark, and in turn the insectivore helps spread the melon's seeds.

An aardvark will claw open a desert melon to drink the water inside the fruit. In so doing, it ingests a number of melon seeds. The undigested seeds are excreted with the animal's dung. Since the aardvark buries its dung, the desert melon seeds find a place in the soil, and a supply of nourishing manure as well!

〜〜〜

Pat Havener packed 90 cans of sardines in 10 minutes

Among the thousands of contests that take place each year, one of the most curious is the World Championship Sardine Packing Contest, which is held every August at Fishermen's Memorial Pier in Rockland, Maine. A regular part of the annual Maine Seafoods Festival, this contest, which reflects the importance of the sardine industry to Maine's economy, attracts numerous entrants from canneries throughout the state.

To pack a sardine, one must pick it up, deftly snip off its head and tail with razor-sharp scissors, and place it neatly in an open sardine can. Whoever packs the most sardines in a 10-minute period receives a cash prize and an engraved trophy from the governor of Maine.

The all-time champion sardine-packer is Mrs. Patricia Havener of Waldoboro, Maine, who, with her mother and sisters, works for the Port Clyde Packing Company in Rockland. In August 1971, when she was 24 years old, Pat Havener packed 90 cans of "number fives" (five sardines to the can) in 10 minutes.

With an overall total of 450 sardines, Pat processed an average of 45 of the shiny little fish each and every minute.

The hippopotamus's sweat is red

The hippopotamus is the second largest land animal in existence, giving precedence only to the elephant. This hefty relative of the hog grows to a length of thirteen feet, and a full-grown hippo can weigh more than six thousand pounds. Yet this African giant is a harmless, playful creature who spends most of his time frisking about in rivers, and never eats anything more than a leaf, root or blade of grass!

Understandably, the hippopotamus rarely gets excited. His great size makes rapid movement impossible, and in any event he is virtually without an enemy in the jungle. But when one of these three-ton titans does become excited, his thick, hairless hide exudes an odd carmine red perspiration that often inspires circus men to promise a "blood-sweating hippo" in their advertisements.

The marmot has an air-raid warning system

High on the slopes of the Rocky Mountains lives a remarkable breed of small, burrowing rodents known as hoary marmots. These furry creatures, each about the size of a rabbit, make their homes in large colonies in the mountains. Each marmot family digs and maintains its own burrow, and a colony can turn a barren, rocky slope into a bustling community. Peer down from the top of one of these slopes and you'll see hundreds of tiny brown heads popping out of holes all across the mountainside.

156

Hoary marmots play happily in the summer sun, nibbling moss and plant rocks, seemingly unconcerned about the danger of predators. But the marmots can afford to be lax in their vigilance. In each colony, one member of the group perches on a high rock and acts as sentinel. At the first glimpse of a dreaded enemy, like the golden eagle, the wary watchguard will fill the air with a thunderous whistle.

Instantly, each marmot scurries for cover in his own burrow. In seconds, a field teeming with busy animals becomes a barren, lifeless mountainside. But then, after the eagle has flown on, another loud whistle breaks the silence—the all-clear signal given by the marmot air-raid warden. And suddenly the slope is alive again.

The whistle of the hoary marmot is an extraordinary sound. Echoing over the rocks and through the valleys, the long, loud shriek sounds like the whistle of a freight train passing in the night. That such a loud sound could come from so small an animal seems unbelievable, for the marmot's voice box is no larger than a peanut. But the cry of this furry little fellow can be heard for a distance of *two miles* in any direction. It is the farthest-reaching sound made by any land animal on earth!

The trap-door spider booby-traps its prey

Spiders have always been known as wily creatures, but the trap-door spider may be the slyest of them all. If you ever catch a glimpse of this crafty critter scurrying over the deserts of Mexico or the southwestern United States, don't be surprised if he disappears before your very eyes!

This amazing arachnid lives in upright tunnels he digs in the parched ground. The mouth of the tunnel is covered with a trap-door that is made of sand and pebbles and hinged to the ground on one side. This door is so skillfully constructed that it's almost impossible to detect when closed. But the trap-door spider knows where the tunnels are, and in a split second he can open the door, slip inside, and close the door again—seemingly vanishing into thin air!

Equally clever is the way the trap-door spider booby-traps his prey. This creature has especially sensitive hearing, and when an unsuspecting insect wanders close to his trapdoor, the spider hears its tread, pops out of his tunnel, and carries his catch inside!

Grunions dance on the beach

Goldfish and tropical fish may keep you amused just by swimming around in their tanks, but there is another species of fish that puts these little entertainers to shame. Grunions, sardine-like fish about five inches long, stage a floor show on the beaches of southern California that might make you think you were watching trained animals in a circus!

Every year in the spring and summer, schools of grunions gather off California's beaches. When the moon and tides are just right, the grunions begin their show. Once carried onto shore by breaking waves, the female stands up on her tail and whirls around in a wild dance! As she dances, her tail digs a small hole in the wet sand. When the hole is deep enough, she deposits her eggs at the bottom.

The male grunion, also swept in by the waves, dances into the holes and fertilizes the eggs. Another wave then carries the male and female back into the ocean. The entire performance lasts only about thirty seconds.

At the next high tide, the rushing waves break the eggs. The newborn grunions then do a short snakedance as they wiggle out to sea. But the following year, the babies will return for an encore, climbing up on the beach to perform the grunion's strange moonlight dance!

◦◦◦

Walcott won the heavyweight boxing title at age 37

A boxer is generally in his prime during his mid-twenties. By the time he has hit twenty-nine he is, as a rule, considered a has-been, ready for retirement.

But not Jersey Joe Walcott. On July 18, 1951, when he entered the ring against the faster, more agile Ezzard Charles, Jersey Joe was challenging the champ for the third time. Twice before, Walcott had tried and lost. Moreover, Walcott had twice lost to former champ Joe Louis. After a total of four failures—in itself a record for trying to take the heavyweight title—Walcott had resigned from the ring.

That Jersey Joe would venture a championship fight for the fifth time was astonishing; and the odds of six to one against him reflected how fistic experts regarded his chances.

Ezzard Charles had seemed a cinch to win. He had come to fight with a string of 24 straight wins behind him. Walcott, the "has-been" and father of six, had gone into the ring with a lot of bills to pay. He had come out of retirement because he needed the money.

The bout was held in Pittsburgh's Forbes Field. A goodly crowd of 28,000 attended and a television audience of 60 million watched. Walcott, 194 pounds, got off to a slow start. But in the third round he opened up a cut under Charles' eye. In the next three rounds, Joe racked up points, and in the seventh, the "old man" lured the champ into a trap. Feinting a body punch, Joe let go with a short, crisp hook—only about six inches—to Charles' jaw. Ezzard fell, tried to rise, then toppled again. The fight was over.

Thus Jersey Joe, a veteran of 21 years in the ring and thirty-seven years old, became the oldest man ever to win the world's heavyweight title.

The anableps has bifocal eyes

A tiny fish called the anableps, which makes its home in the American tropics, has eyes that function just like a pair of bifocal lenses. Each of its eyes is divided into two parts, the upper portion focused for vision above the surface of the water, the lower half for underwater sight. As the anableps swims at the water's surface, it can search for insects on the surface and at the same time watch out below for larger, deeper-swimming fish that would like to munch on the anableps. However, the little fish does have to duck its upper eyes under the water frequently to keep them moist.

Ewry won ten Olympic gold medals

When he was a child growing up in Lafayette, Indiana, Ray Ewry's legs were as wobbly as spaghetti: a case of polio had weakened his limbs. Ray's physician suggested that the lad strengthen his legs through constant jumping exercises.

Ewry followed this advice—and he did so, so perseveringly and so unstintingly, that he actually developed what were perhaps the strongest set of legs in history. In the 1890's, Ewry went to Purdue University where he captained the track team. After he graduated, Ewry earned a place on the United States Olympic team. He was then 26 years old.

On July 16, 1900, in Paris, Ewry won three Olympic gold medals: the standing long jump, the standing high jump, and the standing hop, step and jump—all of which required a stationary start. In the standing high jump Ewry cleared 5 feet, 5 inches, nearly six inches better than his closest competitor.

In the 1904 Olympics, the lanky 6-foot, 3-inch athlete repeated his masterful performance. In 1906 (when a special Olympics was held), and in 1908, Ewry collected medals again for the standing long and high jumps. During a nine-year span, Ray collected 10 Olympic gold medals—no mean accomplishment when it is considered that no athlete, before or since, has won more than seven firsts in Olympic track and field events.

Flying fish use their fins as wings

There are at least sixty-five kinds of "flying fish" found in the oceans of the world—and none are capable of true flight. But these versatile creatures can glide for a considerable distance above the surface of the water, putting on one of nature's most unusual aerial shows.

The flying fish's tail furnishes the driving force required for takeoff. The one-foot-long creature skims along the surface of the water, whipping its tail back and forth to generate speed. When

the fish has developed sufficient takeoff speed, it suddenly spreads its pectoral fins as if they were wings and soars into the air. Once in flight, the fish can bank and maneuver just like an airplane!

The flying fish's average flight lasts only a few seconds, but flights as long as twelve to fourteen seconds have been reported. These graceful creatures shoot out of the water at speeds of up to forty miles an hour, and can glide through the air for distances of up to six hundred feet and more!

Their performances take place at night as well as during the daytime. After dark, many are attracted by lights on ships and—like some birds and insects—fly toward the illumination. Flying fish have been known to crash into a ship's side, land on deck, or even soar through an open porthole!

~~~

Sinclair walked nearly 216 miles without stopping

John Sinclair is the marathon-walking champion of the world, and he has racked up an impressive series of walking records. He walked from John O'Groats in Scotland to Land's End in Cornwall, the length of the island of Britain, about 600 miles, in 19 days and 22 hours. In 1967, he walked from Cape Town to Pretoria, a distance of more than 900 miles, in only 23 days.

But John Sinclair's greatest walking feat was performed between April 21 and 23, 1969. The walk took place at the Wingfield Aerodrome, a facility of the South African Navy just outside Simonstown, and it was conducted under official Navy auspices.

The 50-year-old Sinclair began his record-breaking stroll at 5 p.m. on Tuesday, April 21st. Maintaining a steady pace of four miles an hour, and wearing sturdy leather boots that he had carefully broken in some weeks earlier in preparation for the event, he marched around the field's 5.25-mile perimeter, undaunted by the cold, windy rain that began to fall almost immediately after he started.

The rain continued for the next three days, and so did Sinclair. Officers and enlisted men of the South African Navy provided him with food and drink when needed, and served as official observers to ensure that he kept moving at all times and never varied from the measured course around the field.

John Sinclair made his last circuit around Wingfield Aerodrome at 3:42 p.m. on Thursday, April 23. In 47 hours and 42 minutes, he had walked 215 miles, 1,670 yards—the greatest feat of marathon walking ever recorded.

The birthwort "kidnaps" insects and then sets them free

The flowers of most insect-pollinated plants provide a convenient resting place and nourishing nectar for their welcome insect visitors. Some plants, however, can be rude hosts to the creatures they depend upon for pollination. Among the latter is the birthwort, which lures and then imprisons its insect benefactors, holding the creatures hostage until they've performed their unwitting duty.

Birthwort is the common name for a 600-member family of shrubs and vines most often found in the tropics. Some species are cultivated as medicinals, with their extract used in the treatment of snakebite. Other species, common to the steppes of Western Asia where goats frequently graze, produce flowers that both look and smell like goat droppings!

But the "kidnapper" among the birthwort is a European species. The flower of these plants forms a curving tube similar in shape to a saxophone, which exudes a foul odor attractive to some insects. When a visitor blunders in through the open end of the tube, it quickly becomes a hostage.

Still drawn on by the odor, the insect travels toward the swollen base of the flower tube. Stiff, downward-pointing hairs prevent escape. A transparent area in the wall of the tube, near the base, lures the captive further in search of an exit. Here the insect is likely to brush against the nearby stigma and pollinate the flower.

If the insect doesn't pollinate the flower, it cannot escape. But once the flower has been pollinated, the stigma grows erect and exposes the anthers, which "reward" the insect with a shower of pollen. Then the stiff hairs wither, and the captive is allowed to escape. In some cases, the thankless flower bends downward after pollination and rudely pitches the abused insect out!

The Potala is a palace that is two miles high

Well into this century, Lhasa, the capital of Tibet, was known as the "Forbidden City." In addition to being sealed off from the world by the Himalaya Range and being almost inaccessible by any means of travel, the holy city of Lhasa was closed to foreigners by Tibetan law. For Lhasa has been the home of the Dalai Lama, the spiritual leader of the Tibetan Buddhists. Until recently, few Westerners could claim to have seen Lhasa, or the magnificent palace that overlooks the city: the Potala.

168

Begun in the year 700, the Potala has served through the centuries as the palace of the Dalai Lama, the seat of the Tibetan government, a college, a monastery, and a fort. Lhasa itself is 12,000 feet above sea level, an altitude at which even the hardiest foreigner will find physical activity extremely taxing; yet the Potala was built high above the city, straddling a steep hill just outside Lhasa. Long zig-zagging stairways provide the only access to the fortress.

The Potala—the "Palace of the Gods"—is a massive complex of buildings which extends for 1,000 feet across the side of the hill and rises nine stories over its lofty foundation. More than 1,400 windows look down over the city. Inside, over 1,000 monks can live and study in the Potala's 500 rooms. The quarters of the Dalai Lama are in a smaller palace within the Potala. For the most part, the fortress is white-washed and unornamented, built to withstand the bitter Tibetan winter—but the central portion of the Potala is painted red, and its roof and towers are covered with glittering gold!

Since the Chinese invasion of Tibet in 1959, the Dalai Lama has lived in exile in India. The Potala has been shelled by Chinese troops, and many monks have fled to neighboring Himalayan countries. But in the minds of all Tibetans, the Potala, the palace that soars to the clouds, remains the most sacred building in the world.

<hr />

The cuckoo pint "tars-and-feathers" insects to assure pollination

Most plants that depend upon insects for pollination are gracious hosts, providing their visitors with a convenient passage to and from the nectary. But the cuckoo pint, an arum plant indigenous to Europe, is, on the contrary, quite inhospitable. To assure pollination, the cuckoo pint traps its helpful guests and "tars-and-feathers" the insects before permitting them to depart.

The cuckoo pint generates a fetid odor during the early evening hours, which attracts minute flies that normally breed in cow dung. Mistaking the flower for rotting meat, the flies enter its tubelike chamber and tumble down into the floral trap.

As a fly enters the flower, any pollen it may have picked up from another cuckoo pint is brushed off against the pistil at the bottom of the chamber, thereby pollinating the plant. The fly then gorges itself on a secretion found near the bottom of the pistil. When sated, the fly tries to leave the plant, but the slippery walls of the chamber prevent escape. The prisoner remains, "tarring" itself with the sticky nectar all night long.

In the morning, the stamen further up in the tube trembles lightly and "feathers" the fly with pollen. The flower then wilts and opens slightly, allowing the pollen-laden fly to emerge.

A seal can swim steadily for eight months

Alaskan seals are the best long-distance swimmers in the world. In late spring and summer, they bear their young on the rocky islands off the Alaskan coast. Then they take to the water and swim south to avoid the frigid Arctic winter. For eight months these sleek mammals remain in the ocean, sometimes swimming as much as six thousand miles without once touching land before they return to Alaska in the spring.

Much of these eight months are spent underwater, but unlike most mammals, seals do not have to hold their breaths to prevent themselves from drowning. Like beavers and hippopotamuses, seals have a ringlike muscle around each nostril that can be contracted to prevent water from entering their lungs.

Some cicadas live underground for seventeen years

Cicadas are the loudest singers in the insect world. These large, winged insects snap thin membranes on their thorax to produce a loud chirping that resembles the sound of locusts. In fact, some cicadas are often called "seven-year locusts" or "seventeen-year locusts," though they are not locusts at all.

The latter variety spends seventeen years eating and growing in underground passageways, then emerges for only a few weeks of sunshine before dying. Seventeen years later, a new generation of cicadas will emerge from the ground. These creatures thus constitute the longest-lived species in the insect kingdom!

The Cherry Sisters' terrible acting made them famous and rich

Perhaps the strangest success story in the theatrical world is that of the fabulous Cherry Sisters. Leaving their home in the Iowa corn country in 1893, the four girls made their debut in Cedar Rapids in a skit they wrote themselves. For three years, the Cherry Sisters performed to packed theaters throughout the Middle West; people came to see them just to find out if they really were *that* bad.

Their unbelievably atrocious acting enraged critics and provoked spectators to throw vegetables at the "actresses." Wisely, the sisters thought to travel with an iron screen which they could erect on stage for self-defense.

By 1896, the girls were offered a thousand dollars a week to perform on Broadway.

Seven years later, after the Cherry Sisters had earned the then respectable fortune of $200,000, they retired from theatrical life for the more peaceful life down on the farm. Oddly enough, these successful Broadway "stars" remained convinced to the end that they were truly the most talented actresses to grace the American stage.

Cornflower fruits travel like airborne shuttlecocks

The cornflower, a common herb found throughout much of North America and Europe, has a curious way of dispersing its seeds. The fruits of the cornflower develop in shallow receptacles. Hairlike bristles project from each fruit. In damp weather, these bristles bunch together to form a sort of brush above the receptacle, with the fruits jammed in tightly underneath. In dry weather, the bristles fan out and raise their fruits to the top of the receptacle. Breezes swing the cornflower stalks, and the fruits are tossed into the air like tiny shuttlecocks!

Sigmund swam continuously for 89 hours and 48 minutes

At 7:22 p.m., July 25, 1940, John Sigmund lowered himself into the Mississippi River at St. Louis, Missouri, and set out on one of the most adventuresome swims ever attempted. The 30-year-old St. Louis butcher would swim for 89 hours and 48 minutes before being pulled out of the water on July 28, dazed and exhausted, at Caruthersville, Missouri.

The Mississippi River is so muddy that floating objects often can't be seen. During his stint, Sigmund injured a leg on a submerged log. Some time later, the waves of a passing barge washed him against his accompanying cabin cruiser and nearly knocked him unconscious. And to add to his travail, on the very last night of his journey, Sigmund wandered three miles off course when he mistakenly entered one of the Mississippi's tributaries.

For energy, his wife, Catherine, frequently furnished him with candy bars. It was only through her constant prodding during the final 25 miles that the exhausted Sigmund was prevented from falling asleep in the water. At the finish—292 miles from his starting point, an all-time distance record—hundreds of bystanders cheered. But Sigmund could not acknowledge their acclaim. Unable to either walk or talk, he was carried off by friends.

Nevertheless, the next day John showed no ill effects. The damage—a sun-blistered face, wobbly legs, and aching muscles—would quickly pass away.

Some turtles live for more than 200 years

There is a great deal of truth in the old fable of the hare and the tortoise. The turtle may be one of the slowest creatures in the animal kingdom, but what he lacks in speed he makes up for in longevity. For not only was the turtle thriving long before most of today's animals came into existence, but this cousin of the early dinosaurs lives longer than any other creature on earth! Incredible as it may seem, giant tortoises have been known to attain an age of well over two hundred years, and scientists believe that some turtles may even reach the age of three centuries!

Why does this hard-shelled fellow live so long? Because he takes things easy! A turtle eats slowly, moves slowly, grows slowly, even breathes slowly. It takes more than a year just for the sluggish reptile's shell to become hard. And some turtle eggs take as long as a year to hatch!

176

During his winter hibernation, the turtle's body functions so minimaly he's practically in a state of suspended animation. When winter comes, the cold-blooded creature burrows deep into the mud at the bottom of some body of water—an ocean, lake, river, or pond. His ordinarily slow breathing ceases almost entirely. The tiny amount of oxygen he needs to stay alive is contained in the mud around him. And this mud is also just warm enough to keep him from freezing.

Turtles can be found living both on land and in fresh and salt water, and the marine and terrestrial forms both vary greatly in size. Marine turtles range from just an inch or so up to six feet in length. The Galapagos turtle, a terrestrial species, can weigh up to 500 pounds; but the average adult Leatherback—the largest marine turtle—measures six feet long and weighs 1,000 pounds!

An anaconda can swallow a pig

The gigantic anaconda snake of South America may make do with only one meal in several months, but what a meal it is! This monster of the boa family may range up to twenty-eight feet in length and weigh nearly two hundred pounds, and it is quite capable of swallowing an entire pig or deer.

The anaconda kills by coiling its body around its prey and applying terrific pressure, thereby stopping the victim's heart. Then the snake sets to work swallowing the animal whole, a job that may take several hours. Powerful digestive juices in the serpent's stomach can easily dissolve the largest bones.

The anaconda's huge meal forms a lump that swells the snake out of shape. A hunter who catches one of these snakes soon after a meal can kill the serpent, cut open its body, remove the pig that has just been swallowed, and rush it home to his own cooking pot!

Van den Berg skated 120 miles in seven and a half hours

Ice skating is the favorite winter sport in the Dutch province of Friesland, which since the 18th century has put on the world's longest and most difficult ice skating race.

This race is known as the *Elfstedentocht* ("Eleven Towns Course"), so called because it is skated along the canals, rivers, and lakes connecting the 11 main towns of Friesland. The distance falls just short of 200 kilometers (approximately 124 miles), and the exact course varies somewhat from year to year, depending on ice conditions.

For the *Elfstedentocht* of February 3, 1954, all Dutch soldiers who wanted to skate in the race were given two days leave and free transportation to Leeuwarden, which serves as both starting and finishing point. Even the Dutch Parliament closed down for the day, since one of its most important members announced that he was going to participate.

All told, the 1954 *Elfstedentocht* attracted 138 formal contenders. In addition, as has always been the custom, there were several thousand other skaters who came out to skate the full distance at a more leisurely pace, without any thought of competing.

The winner of this ice-skating marathon was a young schoolteacher from the town of Nijbeets in Friesland, one Jeen van den Berg, who at the time was 26 years old. He covered the 124-mile distance in 7 hours 35 minutes, besting the previous record for the grueling course by more than an hour, and becoming a national hero in the process.

The otter can dodge a rifle bullet

The otter, a member of the weasel family, makes his home on the banks of northern lakes and streams. This frisky fellow resembles a small seal, with a sleek, streamlined body, webbed hind feet, and a long, flat tail he uses as a rudder in swimming. An otter will often share a river bank with a beaver, but the two animals are as different as night and day: While the beaver is a hard-working, industrious sort, the otter is a fun loving fellow, one of the most playful of all animals—and one of the quickest!

Beavers spend a good deal of their day constructing dams, but otters prefer to spend their time building slides on the slopes of a snowy hill. Their favorite game is belly whopping. Their smooth stomachs are better to slide on than a toboggan, and their flat tails serve as steering gear. When the otters reach the bottom of the hill they wait for their playmates to take their slides. Then they all scurry back up to the top of the hill, take a short run, and belly whop down again. Best of all, otters love to slide down a hill right into the water!

For quickness, few animals can match the otter. In the water, this playboy of the animal world moves like greased lightning. He can poke his head out of a hole in the ice, disappear, and pop up through another hole yards away in a matter of seconds. And many hunters have reported that they've fired at an otter as he poked through an ice-hole, only to watch the creature disappear into the water again unharmed—*before* the bullet could reach the hole. The otter is indeed "faster than a speeding bullet"!

The towers of the Shwe Dagon Pagoda
are completely covered with gold

Each year, thousands of Burmese pilgrims journey to the capital city of Rangoon to visit the country's most sacred temple, the Shwe Dagon Pagoda. This 15th century temple-monastery, the center of all Burmese religious life, is most notable for its tall, cone-shaped towers, which are completely covered with gold.

Shwe Dagon is a complex of temples, reliquaries, towers, and gates, abounding in richly carved ornamentation. Surrounding the complex is a multi-colored tiled terrace 1,420 feet around. Towering above the terrace and gateways are the brick stupas, or sacred relic chambers, each of which is surmounted by a cone-shaped tower covered with gold leaf. The largest of these towers is 326 feet above the terrace, and its glittering gold pinnacle can be seen from virtually any part of Rangoon.

Through the ages, while Western churches have been pillaged, the Pyramids looted, and the Taj Mahal stripped of its gems, here in the center of a large city a fortune in gold has remained untouched. Neither an earthquake that ravaged the city, nor floods, nor heavy bombardment during the Second World War could destroy the fabulous golden cones of Shwe Dagon.

⌘

The smallest flowering plant is one seventy-millionth the size of the largest

The smallest flowering plants in the world are the Wolffia and Wolffiella that make up the green film seen on many fresh-water ponds. These aquatic midgets, known also as duckweed and watermeal, range in diameter from one-thirtieth to a mere one-fifieth of an inch. Compare these plants to the mammoth *Amorphophallus titanum,* one of the world's largest flowering plants: the duckweed is but one seventy-millionth as large!

⌘

The resurrection plant moves in search of water

The resurrection plant, a desert growth found in arid regions of America and the Near East, owes its name to its extraordinary ability to come to life again from a seemingly dead and shriveled state. Of course, the plant does not really come back from the dead, but from a form of "hibernation" in which it is almost completely inactive. And unlike most other plants, which must wait for water, the resurrection plant can move over the land to search for needed moisture!

The name *resurrection plant* is applied to several species, including the Biblical rose of Jericho, which exhibit similar resurrective powers. In the presence of water, a resurrection plant will flourish, sporting green fernlike leaves. But when moisture is scarce, the plant pulls up its roots and withers into a dry, ball-like

183

mass of apparently dead matter, completely devoid of green coloration. This withered mass is carried along the ground by the
wind, and can remain in a dormant state *for years* if no water is
found!

But once moisture is located, or after a rain, the plant sinks roots
into the wet ground and springs to life again. Its leaves uncurl,
again revealing green tissue on their undersides. The plant fares
well until the moisture has evaporated, then curls up into a withered ball and roams again in search of water!

Robert Earl Hughes was the fattest man who ever lived

In 1926, a bouncing 11½-pound boy was born into the Hughes
family of Fish Hook, Illinois. Christened Robert Earl, this Hughes
boy was obviously bound for big things. At the age of six, he
tipped the scales at 203 pounds; four years later, he weighed 378.
He didn't stop adding avoirdupois until he had nearly tripled that
weight.

In the last year of his life, spent with a touring carnival, Hughes
had his dimensions reliably measured. His weight was 1,069

pounds; his waist was 124 inches around, exceeding the measure of his chest by two inches.

In July of 1958, Hughes came down with a case of measles. Though Hughes was gravely ill, he could not enter the hospital in Bremen, Indiana, where the carnival had stopped, for he could not pass through its door. Hughes' specially built house trailer was kept in the hospital parking lot, where oxygen could be administered and doctors and nurses could check on him.

All this attention proved to no avail. The measles cleared up, but were immediately followed by uremia—a failure of the kidneys. Robert Earl Hughes passed away on July 10, 1958. His coffin was made from a piano case, transported to a cemetery in Mount Sterling, Illinois, via a moving van. The weight of the coffin plus its occupant was over a ton; Hughes had to be lowered into the earth by a crane.

There is another American who is reputed to have weighed more than Hughes. Johnny Alee of Carbon, North Carolina (1853-1887), allegedly tipped the scales at 1,132 pounds, However, no reliable verification of this figure exists.

Kangaroos can't walk—but they can travel at 40 miles an hour

The kangaroo is undoubtedly the world's champion jumper. This curious-looking Australian mammal cannot walk at all—but he sure can leap! Moving along in fifteen- to twenty-foot bounds, a racing kangaroo can travel at close to forty miles an hour. And he can leap without stopping for hours at a time, sometimes covering a distance of twenty miles without a rest!

The kangaroo has a small head and large pointed ears, like a rabbit's. His front limbs are very short, but his hind quarters are the size of a mule's, with feet that sometimes measure ten inches from the heel to the longest toe. The kangaroo's thick tail is so strong that he can sit on it as if it were a stool. Big feet give the kangaroo a firm grounding, and his strong tail helps him keep his balance during long leaps. Although he is no taller than five feet, this bouncy fellow can easily hop over a parked car!

The kangaroo is a marsupial, which means that the female has a pouch for transporting her offspring. After birth, an infant kangaroo—only an inch long—is immediately placed in this fur-lined pouch, outside his mother's stomach, where he nurses cozily for four to five months. This arrangement is convenient for the parent, too, because she can go about her business without taking time out to look after her baby. When the young kangaroo grows too large to fit into the pouch, he leaves his snug retreat and learns to leap like his parents.

The kangaroo is a vegetarian, and will seldom harm another animal. But the big bouncers can be trained to box with boxing gloves, just like prizefighters. The kangaroo will use his two front paws to hit, swing, and deliver some surprisingly solid blows. His tail acts as a third leg, and gives him extra support. A trained kangaroo will stay on his feet long after his boxing partner is exhausted!

Browning somersaulted seven feet and three inches

In 1954, the world's record for the high jump was six feet, eleven and one-half inches, held by Walt Davis who was almost that tall himself. But that year there was a little five-foot nine-inch gymnast who could leap even higher.

Dick Browning, a 20-year-old sophomore of the University of Illinois, was generally acknowledged to be the world's greatest tumbler at the time. His execution of the somersault was nonpareil. He was so good he could beat the best high jumper of his day.

188

On April 27, 1954, at an exhibition in Santa Barbara, California, Dick Browning, rounding off his routine, somersaulted over a bar which was seven feet, three inches high. When Browning's record was reported, track coaches all over the country scoffed. Track rules specifically insist that a high jump be executed from a one-foot take-off. If this five-foot nine-inch midget did in fact leap seven feet, then he must have, they claimed, pushed off with two feet. However, all who had been present and carefully watched the performance avowed that when Browning took off, he had turned his body slightly in order to get more spring, and that, in fact, one of his feet left the ground before the other. Dick's leap, witnesses insisted, complied with all the rules.

Whether the jump was or was not according to Hoyle is really beside the point. For the wonder still stands: how could a man execute a somersault so high that he indeed did clear a seven-foot three-inch bar?

A pit viper finds its food by radar

Three poisonous snakes indigenous to the United States—the rattlesnake, copperhead, and water moccasin—all belong to a family of snakes known as the pit vipers. These creatures are probably the most recently evolved of all snakes, for they are equipped with not only venomous fangs, but a sort of radar system as well.

The pit vipers have a small hole, or *pit*, behind each nostril. This depression, which looks very much like a second nostril, is actually a sixth sense, a kind of radar organ sensitive to heat rays. By using this unusual organ a pit viper can find its prey—even in the dark—by following the body heat radiated by the victim's body!

Nilsson crossed the United States on a unicycle

Walter Nilsson was a vaudeville performer who was touted on the stage as "The King of the Unicycles." In 1934, Nilsson proved that his star billing was entirely justified. In those days, Robert Ripley, creator of *Believe It or Not* books, was in great vogue. He actually ran an annual contest to encourage daredevils and weirdos to attempt strange feats. Nilsson decided to get into the act. Accompanied by a representative of the Ripley organization, Nilsson left New York with intent to travel, by unicycle, to California, a distance of 3,306 miles.

Poised on top of an 8½-foot high contraption, Walter began his strange trek. Though the ride was painful, and Nilsson developed physical ailments that would bother him for the rest of his life, never once did the 33-year-old actor fall off his bike. Some 117 days after he left New York, Nilsson pedaled into San Francisco to earn a hero's welcome and win Ripley's award as having pulled off "The Most Unbelievable Feat of the Year."

A 40-pound wolverine can kill a 300-pound caribou

The wolverine is the largest and fiercest member of the weasel family. This furry resident of the northern regions is a savage hunter, stalking its prey and then leaping from a rock or tree for the kill. Although the wolverine is usually less than four feet long, and weighs only forty pounds or so, this ravenous creature will attack almost any animal it meets—even a three-hundred-pound caribou!

The wolverine is as cunning as it is vicious, and will rob the most cleverly constructed traps. It can, in the words of one trapper, dig like a badger, climb like a squirrel, swim like an otter, and jump to the height of a man.

French-Canadians call the wolverine *carcajou*—glutton—because it will gorge itself on almost anything. But this fierce little fellow will never attack a man.

Victoria Zacchini traveled 200 feet as a human cannonball

Few circus events require the daring and poise of the stunt which has become to be known as "The Human Cannonball." This act employs lots of phony noise and smoke, and then jets a human being into space from the mouth of a cannon.

Despite the hoopla, the successful completion of this act depends on exact coordination between the person who is being shot, the huge spring that catapults him, and the assistants in charge of the mechanism. The "cannonball" must maintain his

poise while traveling through the air—and he travels faster than a speeding automobile. He is supposed to land in a net some distance away, but if the propulsion is weak or there is some other flaw, he can fall short of that distance with disastrous results. Over 30 human "bullets" have died during the 20th century.

During April of 1943, in New York's Polo Grounds, Victoria Zacchini was shot from the barrel of the 22-foot silver cannon at a speed of well over 100 miles an hour. The 110-pound human projectile climbed to a height of over 100 feet and then fell safely into a net 200 feet away—a record shot!

The Egyptian bean germinates while floating

The seeds of the Egyptian bean, or Indian lotus, enjoy a short river cruise before settling down to grow. This pink-blossomed plant, sacred to the Hindu and Buddhist alike, takes root in the silt of a river bottom, with its stalk extending upwards through the water. The fruits develop in large woody receptacles attached to the stalk at water level. Each receptacle normally contains from 20 to 25 individual sockets, with one fruit in each socket.

When the seeds are ripe, the receptacle breaks off from the stalk and the woody ark begins floating downstream. During their journey, the seeds begin to germinate, sending out shoots and leaves that give the water-borne seed pod the appearance of a floating flower pot. Eventually, the sprouted fruits are dislodged from the pod and sink to the bottom of the river, where the new plants will grow.

~~~✦~~~

The honeybee's wings beat two hundred times per second

A honeybee hive is one of the busiest places in the world, a crowded city literally buzzing with activity. In the fifty thousand rooms, or cells, of an average beehive, more than 35,000 bees go about their never-ending labors, each performing a special job.

There is the queen, who lays her own weight in eggs daily; there are drones, male bees whose only task is to mate with newly hatched queens; there are workers, females who serve as nurses, guards, cell builders, and food gatherers for the insect metropolis. These bees leave the hive to seek the flower nectar with which they manufacture honey and wax for the colony. And it's hard work—it takes 37,000 trips from hive to flower and back again to produce just one pound of honey!

But bees are quick and thrive on constant work. Their frail wings beat at the incredible rate of two hundred times per second! That's so fast that the human eye perceives only a blur—and some cameras do, too!

The bee's rapid wing beat is put to another use when the insects are in their hive. Since it is difficult for fresh air to reach all the workers and young bees in the middle of a hive, the resident bees set up an air-conditioning system, beating their wings to create a draft. In the winter, this activity keeps the bees warm.

Incidentally, bees are unaware of the buzzing sound they're noted for. As far as anyone can tell, honeybees are completely deaf.

Mary Joyce traveled 1,000 miles by dog sled

The rigors of the frozen North are famed in song and story. A dog-sled trip of even 100 miles holds its terrors for even a strong man enured to the biting cold and fierce winds of the frigid zone.

Yet on Thursday, March 26, 1936, in the dead of the Arctic winter, one 27-year-old Alaskan girl drove her dog sled into Fairbanks, Alaska, from distant Taku—a trip of 1,000 miles. She had left her hunting lodge which was 40 miles from Juneau on Decem-

ber 22, 1935, heading into the treacherous mountains, the blizzards, and the loneliness which lay ahead. For about three months, without any human aid, she battled the elements, rarely encountering weather any milder than 34 degrees below zero, and hitting days when the thermometer dropped to 60 below.

Neatly attired in dark blue hiking trousers, heavy blue woolen jacket, snug-fitting black fur cap and knee-length moccasins, Miss Joyce presented a striking picture as she swung down the home stretch of the Richardson Highway into Fairbanks, where standing exultantly in front of her team of five huskies, she was acclaimed by the town's notables.

Kittinger dropped 16 miles before opening his parachute

Inscribed on the cockpit door of the balloon was a legend that read: "The world's biggest step." And indeed it was! For the balloon carrying Joseph Kittinger, a United States Air Force captain, was 19 miles up in the sky, sailing along at a height of 102,000 feet over New Mexico, when on August 16, 1960, Kittinger took that step, and made history.

Falling freely through the air, Kittinger picked up speed each second. Mile after mile he fell, with his parachute firmly packed on his back. But though he encountered a pitiless wind as he reached a falling speed of over 600 miles an hour, the 32-year-old Kittinger maintained his composure. It wasn't easy to brook a temperature as low, at times, as 94 degrees below zero.

Yet, before releasing his chute, the dauntless captain dropped 84,700 feet—more than 16 miles! He had fallen through space for four minutes and 38 seconds, a world's record for a free fall.

After Kittinger opened his parachute, it took 13 minutes for him to float down the last three miles to terra firma.

**Ross paddled across the English Channel
in four hours and seven minutes**

The kayak was invented by the Eskimos for hunting trips in the
stilled icy seas of the Far North. Certainly this rather frail craft
was not conceived to battle the churning swells and tidal currents
of the English Channel. But civilized man, in order to evidence his
mastery of nature, has always sought new ways to pit brain and
muscle against seemingly unconquerable forces. And so the men
of our day have taken to cross the Channel in kayaks. The fact is
it's been done several times.

In this exercise, none was faster than one Henry Ross, an engi-
neer from Surrey, England. Setting out from Gris Nez in France
on a bright morning, August 10, 1950, Ross began to paddle
toward Dover. It was the same 22-mile route taken by most Channel swimmers.

Aided by ideal weather and driven by furious determination, the 37-year-old Ross moved much faster than even he had planned. When he pullled into Dover only four hours and seven minutes after leaving France, he learned that he had bested the then existing record by a full 50 minutes.

William Northmore lost $850,000 on the turn of a card

William Northmore (1690-1735) of Okehampton, England, was an inveterate gambler. Cards were what he loved best, but he'd just as soon bet on the horses, or on votes in Parliament.

After several years of stunning success, he met his downfall in the form of an ace of diamonds. With the turn of that one card, his entire fortune of $850,000 was wiped out. Northmore vowed never to gamble another penny, but his promise was somewhat hollow, for he had nary a penny to gamble with.

Lady Luck soon smiled on the beggared young man, not at the gaming tables, but at the polls. The townspeople of Okehampton, in sympathy for Northmore's plight, elected him to Parliament in 1714, and in every election thereafter until his death 19 years later.

The llama spits when angry

Of all man's beasts of burden, only the llama is capable of carrying loads at very high altitudes. In the thin, freezing air of South America's Andes Mountains, this woolly camel is indispensable to the Indians who reside there. He carries their burdens along the treacherous slopes, provides wool for clothing, and blankets and milk for Indian children. The llama's manure, when dried in the sun, provides the Indians with their only fuel. And when the beast dies, he is used to make leather.

But the llama, unlike the horse, simply refuses to be overworked. Knowing to the ounce just how much he can carry comfortably, the shaggy-haired carrier will drop to the ground and refuse to budge if so much as an extra pound is placed on his back. Furthermore, the llama will carry a burden only so far. After about twenty miles the arrogant fellow will begin a determined sit-down strike. Once the llama has decided to stop working, he can't be coaxed.

And what if an inexperienced master tries to make his llama work after the animal has decided to call it quits? Well, that man is in for an unpleasant surprise. An angry llama puckers his lips and spits in his tormentor's face—shooting a vile green juice from his mouth with surefire accuracy!